This book is dedicated to my newborn daughter Jasmine and her fantastic father Stefan. You mean everything to me!

ELIQ MARANIK

VEGAN SMOOTHIES

Natural and energizing drinks for all tastes

*h.f.*ullmann

TABLE OF CONTENTS

Foreword 7

Introduction 9

Getting started 11
Choosing your fruit and vegetables 11
Ripe or unripe 11
Rinse off sprays 12
To peel or not to peel 12
Pits 12
Preparing and freezing fruit 12
Blender or juicer 13
Organically grown fruit 13
Ethylene gas 13
Be creative 14
Why make your own smoothies? 14
Bought smoothies 14
Serving and decorating 15

The utensils you will need 17
Useful equipment 18

Tips and advice 21
Boost the nutritional content 21
Toning down the flavor 21
Enhancing the flavor 21
Thinner smoothies 21
Thicker smoothies 21
Smoother smoothies 22
Chilled smoothies 22
Popsicles made from smoothies 22

Serve immediately 22
Decoration 22
Create your own recipes 22

Ingredients 25
A guide to fruit and vegetables 25
Frozen fruit and berry fruit 30
Dried fruit 30
Preserved fruit 30
Berry powder 30

Give your smoothie a boost 33
Superfoods and super berries 33
Sweeteners 35
Nut butter 35
Seaweed 35
Protein powder 35
Healthy oils 35
Nutritious flavorings 36
Liquid bases 37
Nuts and seeds 39
Make your own nut milk 40

Smoothie recipes 42
Light & fruity smoothies 42
Rich & creamy smoothies 97
Green smoothies 129

Glossary 140

Index of recipes 142

FOREWORD

BOOST YOUR BODY WITH VITAMINS, MINERALS, AND ANTIOXIDANTS!

Breakfast blues—start the day with a nutritious vitamin kick. Want to lose some weight—try smoothies. Tired and listless—give yourself a lift with an energy bomb. Stressed and short of time—drink a "quick fix" smoothie. Exhausted after a session at the gym—give your body renewed strength. Diet low in proteins—top up your reserves.

Regardless of the need, there are vegan smoothies for almost every one of them. A well-formulated smoothie is stimulating, cleansing, and restorative, and helps to stabilize your weight. The body is strengthened and your feeling of wellbeing increases.

In every age people have eaten fruit and vegetables to feel good, but today most people eat far too little of the substances the body needs to maintain good health and vitality.

The book you are holding in your hand contains about fifty recipes for easy-to-make vegan smoothies that will make you feel good and maintain your body's equilibrium. There are drinks here for every taste. Energy-rich fruits are mixed with nutritious fiber, seed, and nut oils, all kinds of nuts and seeds, algae, super berry powders, and other natural food supplements. Try a spinach apple smoothie, a mango, orange & rose hip smoothie—or why not a carrot, pineapple & goji berries smoothie?

The book also includes practical and factual advice on how fruit, vegetables, nuts, food supplements, and other ingredients should be stored; what health benefits they offer; what can be frozen; what pitfalls to avoid in food shops; and a lot of other things that are useful for you to know.

Treat yourself to a richer and healthier life!

Eliq Maranik

INTRODUCTION

WHY VEGAN?

Vegan—the word means more than just the rejection of products of animal origin. For many people it has become a lifestyle choice to feed solely on plants. Saving animals from exploitation is one part of this, and so are issues of climate protection and feeding the world. In comparison with many plant foods, animal products are associated with significantly higher energy consumption. About one third of the contribution that a family makes to global warming is caused by their food!

Not least however there are also health aspects that are making the vegan diet increasingly popular. Even a short term change may achieve miracles in terms of wellbeing. People feel fitter and have more energy.

Eating a vegan diet does not just mean giving up meat and fish, but giving up any animal product, which includes for instance milk, eggs, and honey. The substances that these foods contain—some of which are important to the body—often can be replaced with alternative foods. With a strict vegan diet, great care should be taken to ensure an adequate supply of iron, calcium, iodine, zinc, and Vitamin B12.

However, anyone who chiefly associates a vegan diet with giving things up will learn better in this book. There is a large range of delicious foods that is suitable for vegans. Many of them are presented on pages 25 to 40, with details of what they contain and how they can be used.

WHY SMOOTHIES?

Nowadays it is almost impossible to imagine the vegan kitchen without smoothies. Through their con-centrated wealth of vitamins, minerals, and fiber, plus secondary plant substances, they can completely replace a whole raw food meal in the twinkling of an eye, and the ease of transporting them makes them perfect for a vegan diet in the workplace. The wealth of variations means it is possible to enjoy satisfying smoothies every day, for breakfast and also for lunch and dinner—and completely without having a guilty conscience. Thanks to their smooth consistency these colorful all-rounders made from fresh, natural, and seasonally variable ingredients are not only beneficial and easily digested, but also extremely health-giving thanks to their wealth of vital substances. They are thought to lower the risk of developing diet-related diabetes, high blood pressure, or suffering a heart attack. For people who "don't do" mornings they are particularly important: they provide energy for the whole day! A lot of people therefore choose smoothies as a healthy substitute for coffee. No wonder then that even non-vegans long ago discovered for them-selves this delicious, low-fat drink. Children too love the colorful mixtures of fruit and vegetables.

GETTING STARTED

CHOOSING YOUR FRUIT AND VEGETABLES

The key to success with smoothies begins at the fruit and vegetable counter—learning to find, choose, store, and use the right seasonal raw ingredients is the secret to success for a smoothie enthusiast. The most important thing in finding the best possible ingredients is to use your eyes, nose, and fingers, and as far as possible to buy organic local produce. For the best results, choose fruit and vegetables according to the season. Fresh and freshly picked fruit produces a wonderful, intense flavor, while fruit that has been picked before it is ripe and then transported for miles often produces a very watery and dull result.

Local markets and farm shops are the best places if you want to find really fresh fruit and vegetables. What they sell has not been harvested unripe in order to survive a long journey. What is more, this produce is often cheaper than in food stores.

Take your time when you are choosing. Only buy fruit and vegetables that you are going to use within a few days. Don't stock up, unless you are thinking of freezing them; fresh raw produce is spoiled by being kept.

Try to find highly colored, bright, firm, aromatic specimens with no soft spots or discoloration. It is better to pick them out for yourself than to buy them ready packed because it can be difficult to judge the quality of the latter. It is also important to store fruit and vegetables correctly so that they stay fresh at home. Don't forget that some kinds of fruit should not be stored close to others.

Tests have shown that a lot of fruit and vegetables that are sold in shops contain traces of pesticides— so choose primarily the organic alternative. Organically grown fruit is completely without additives, unsprayed, and has a softer skin and much more flavor. In the shop organic produce is a little more expensive than the conventionally grown but it is worth the difference in price. It is a good idea to try different kinds, both organic and conventionally grown, and learn by tasting. It is fun to compare and find your own favorites. I make a note of taste impressions and log comments in a notebook, which has helped me a lot in finding my own favorite varieties.

Unfortunately the name of the variety of, for instance, the mango or the orange on sale in the shop is not always shown, which makes it harder to know what you are buying. Be prepared to make a nuisance of yourself and ask! If the person you ask can't answer all your questions, ask to speak to someone who can— someone in the shop should know since all deliveries should be marked with that kind of information.

There are also many helpful companies that deliver fruit and vegetables directly to your door. They usually reveal where the fruit comes from, what variety it is, and sometimes even give details of the grower.

RIPE OR UNRIPE

In order to ensure that your smoothie has a good flavor and consistency, it is important to choose fruit that is just right. Unripe fruit is both more sour and harder, and it lacks that little extra something. Overripe fruit is often too sweet—sometimes it has even gone off—and then the smoothie becomes nauseating since the flavors become concentrated when the fruit is pulped. Overripe bananas, peaches, and mangos do not produce a pleasant flavor. Choose fruit that feels heavy for its size and has a strong aroma—usually a sign that it is ripe. Most fruit continues to ripen at room temperature after it has been picked. Some become both sweeter and juicier with time; some become juicier but not sweeter.

RINSING OFF SPRAYS

Whenever fruit and vegetables are not picked in your own garden, you don't know how they have been treated, where they have been stored, or who has touched them—nor do you know about spraying and waxing. Most fruit and vegetables, especially imported produce, are sprayed to give them a longer shelf-life. Therefore it is extremely important to wash and brush them properly. The ones that are not organic should also be peeled—otherwise everything that is on the skin will end up in your body.

The easiest way is to wash all hard fruit and vegetables thoroughly in tepid water, using a soft vegetable brush. Do not use the brush for any other purpose and wash it thoroughly each time you have used it. You can wash soft fruit in warm or tepid water and rub it with your hands or the soft side of a dishwashing sponge (which must also be used only for washing fruit). Citrus fruit and fruit that has a very hard waxed surface can be washed with a little unperfumed, organic dishwashing liquid and a soft sponge. Don't forget to rinse the fruit well always after you have used dishwashing liquid.

There are also special organic fruit washing liquids that ensure that the wax and dirt is removed from the surface of the skin. An alternative is to squeeze half a lemon into tepid water and leave the fruit to soak in it for a few minutes before you brush it.

It is safest to peel nonorganic fruit as well. Even fruit with peel that is not eaten—such as bananas, oranges, mandarins, melons, mangos, and so on—should be washed since pesticides and wax stick to the hands and are then transmitted when you handle the flesh of the fruit.

TO PEEL OR NOT TO PEEL

Most of the vitamins, minerals, and enzymes are located just under the skin or in it. If you use organic produce you should therefore leave the skin on—but always wash fruit and vegetables thoroughly in warm water. Nonorganic fruit should be peeled as thinly as possible, even if it is only going to be squeezed. Always peel bananas, mangos, pineapple, papaya, and avocados. On the other hand kiwifruit do not always need to be peeled—if they are to be put through a juicer the peel can be left on, but if they are to be blended it is best to remove the peel first.

You can leave the skin on unwaxed citrus fruit provided they are not to be put through the juicer or the blender. For smoothies it is best to remove peel and pits that are too hard because small pieces of them may produce an uneven consistency.

PITS

Remove the big pits from mangos, avocados, nectarines, peaches, plums, apricots, and other drupes. Soft pits and seeds can perfectly well go in the juicer or blender, but I usually remove them because they give a certain taste and they affect the consistency.

Dark seeds, for example in watermelon and passion fruit, give the smoothie a rather grayish color but also contain some nutrients. A low powered blender or hand-held blender may have difficulty in pulverizing the seeds, and in that case they can be removed. Always remove the seeds from papaya since their seeds are peppery and impart a strong flavor to the smoothie.

PREPARING AND FREEZING FRUIT

Don't cut the fruit and vegetables up too far ahead. In contact with the air a lot of nutrients, vitamins, minerals, and enzymes begin to oxidize and decompose after a while.

If you make smoothies often and in large quantities, it is a good idea to buy masses of fruit when it is in season and freeze it. Even though fresh produce is always best, frozen fruit is preferable to fruit that is unripe or stale. For example fresh soft fruit such as strawberries, raspberries, and blueberries only keep for a day or two after they have been picked.

Wash, peel, and cut the fruit into pieces before you freeze it. Pack portions in freezer bags with one or more types of fruit in each. Sealable bags that are airtight are best. Try to squeeze as much air as possible out of the bags before you close them. Mark them with the date, the number of portions, and the contents. Fruit keeps for at least two to three months in a home freezer.

To avoid the fruit forming big lumps you can spread it out first on a small baking tray in the freezer, before you pack it in the freezer bags. That way the pieces stay separate and you don't need to thaw a whole bag at a time or struggle to separate them before you blend them. It is particularly useful to freeze bananas, mangos, papaya, pineapple, pomegranate seeds, cherries, rhubarb, and small soft fruit in this way.

When you make smoothies fruit can either be thawed a little beforehand or—depending on the strength of the blender—blended directly. If you want to make juice, small berry fruit should be completely thawed, otherwise it can be difficult to get the liquid out of them.

BLENDER OR JUICER
Hard fruit and vegetables, for example apples and pears, benefit from being pressed in a juicer before they are blended. A powerful blender, like my *Vitamix*, can press and blend at the same time without losing any fiber or producing a stringy consistency. If you have a smaller blender on the other hand, it is best to use the juicer first and then blend the flesh and the juice of the fruit to make the smoothie. Note that you do not get any juice from bananas or avocados, instead they are blended to a purée. Soft fruit such as drupes, berries, and tropical fruit are perfect to put through a blender directly. They turn into smooth juicy purées while at the same time keeping all their nutritional value.

Always wash up the juicer and the blender immediately after you have used them. Clean them with a soft brush that is used only for fruit and vegetables (a brush is often supplied with the blender).

ORGANICALLY GROWN FRUIT
Organic fruit and vegetables are harvested when they are relatively ripe. That way they have a lower water content, smell stronger, taste better, and are juicier and more nutritious than conventionally grown fruit. On the other hand, they have a slightly shorter shelf-life, are more sensitive, and may have flaws. Blemishes occur because organic fruit do not contain any preservatives or artificial additives and are not sprayed with chemical fungicides, wax—or other substances—to make them keep longer, look shinier, and keep their color and shape.

Organic fruit can benefit from being stored in a cool dark place to give them a better shelf-life and flavor, and they should be eaten relatively soon after purchase.

Organic fruit and vegetables contain more vitamins, minerals, enzymes, and other nutrients than conventionally grown ones. Among other things, they have higher levels of vitamin C and antioxidants (for example vitamin E and carotenoids) that protect us against a series of cardiac and vascular diseases.

ETHYLENE GAS
Some fruit and vegetables produce ethylene gas, a substance that accelerates both their own and other fruit's ripening process. Apples, pears, melons, bananas, peaches, nectarines, plums, apricots, and tomatoes give off a lot of ethylene gas, and should therefore not be stored together with other fruit and vegetables—which might otherwise shrivel, get a funny taste, or become overripe. Bananas, mangos, and avocados particularly can ripen far too quickly if they are placed close to other fruit that gives off ethylene gas.

On the other hand, you can take advantage of the ethylene gas if you want unripe fruit and vegetables to ripen more quickly. In that case place them in a bowl or a bag with a fruit that gives off a lot of ethylene gas and the process will happen more quickly.

BE CREATIVE

Don't be afraid to invent your own recipes, but remember not to mix too many different fruit or too many strong flavors in one and the same smoothie. Bland juice from apples, pears, carrots, and oranges goes well with most other fruit and vegetables. If you use fruit with a strong or bitter flavor you can sweeten the smoothie with a bland juice.

Vegetables may not initially be associated with smoothies, but they can be used in moderate quantities too. For example press beets, chili, spinach, celery, bell peppers, or broccoli in a juicer and pulp them.

You can also work with different herbs, powdered berries, or seaweed, nuts, seeds, protein powder, dried berries, and natural fibers that are available in health food shops and delicatessens. And don't forget the garnish! Make your own creations and let your imagination flow.

WHY MAKE YOUR OWN SMOOTHIES?

In my local food shop nowadays there are loads of readymade smoothies and juices for sale, so why make things complicated with cumbersome machines, heavy bags of food, and an unnecessary waste of time to make your own smoothies? For me the answer is simple: it is fun, it is easy, it is delicious, and my body feels good on it!

The advantage of pressing your own juice and mixing your own smoothies is also that you know precisely what they contain. You can choose the fruit and vegetables yourself, and that way you make sure that you always have the freshest and finest ingredients. You can also easily adjust the ingredients and proportions to your favorite flavors. The possibilities of inventing new recipes are endless and once you have started it is hard to stop.

A lot of cafés have started serving freshly pressed juices and smoothies, which is great since you can easily get something nutritious instead of a latte and a pastry. But make sure you ask about the ingredients, whether they use sugar or other sweeteners, and whether your smoothie or juice is freshly made. Don't hesitate to ask the staff about what the smoothie contains and when the fruit that has been used was cut up. In a really good place you can see when the fruit is cut up—and maybe even get to choose the fruit yourself as well.

BOUGHT SMOOTHIES

There are a lot of reputable and committed companies that supply good healthy smoothies to the shops for those occasions when you can't, don't have time to, or don't want to make your own. These smoothies have 100 percent fruit content—with no additives, flavor enhancers, colorants, sweeteners, or concentrates. Buying that kind of smoothie is definitely a good option but it can never match up to a freshly made smoothie of newly cut-up, fresh fruit that you drink straight after making it. Beware of smoothies that contain colorants, flavor enhancers, sweeteners, concentrates, and other added substances. The list of ingredients should preferably contain nothing but fruit.

SERVING AND DECORATING

For me it is really important that what I eat and drink should look appetizing—all my senses should be stimulated. That is why I like to serve smoothies in attractive glasses that I decorate with fresh fruit, vegetables, herbs, edible flowers, and anything else I can find that is fun. There are endless ways of decorating and serving smoothies or juices; just look at cocktails and let their fantastic decorations and fun presentation inspire you.

It can also be fun to use ice as a decoration. You can buy molds in craft shops to make imaginative ice shapes. In addition you can freeze small berry fruit, edible flowers, or herbs in ice cubes to make the decoration extra delightful. I often save quirky cocktail stirrers when I am on my travels and use them to decorate my smoothies and juices.

Children, who can often be hard to please when it comes to fruit and green vegetables, think it is cool and delicious to drink smoothies—especially if they are allowed to come shopping and choose the ingredients, make them, and decorate them. If you want to have even more fun with the children (or your adult friends) you can freeze smoothies in ice cream molds with sticks—nutritious and delicious! But don't keep smoothie ices too long in the freezer, they can become mushy and they will not be nearly so delicious.

Every health drink should look so good that it is hard to resist. Personally I like to serve smoothies in beautiful glasses with attractive decorations.

THE UTENSILS YOU WILL NEED

To prepare smoothies you don't really need anything more than a sharp knife and a blender, but there are a lot of utensils that make the work easier and make the results both tastier and more elegant.

BLENDER. This is a must for making smoothies. A hand-held blender with its own bowl also works well but I recommend investing in a proper blender with a jug. They are more fun and easier to work with. Pour all the ingredients in, press the button, and the smoothie is ready to serve. Blenders are sometimes called *mixers*.

There are a few things to think about when you are choosing a blender, for example how powerful the motor is, how many speeds it has, how much it can hold, and whether it can crush ice. I recommend a blender with a glass jug as they are more robust, easier to keep clean, and not as easily scratched or discolored as the plastic ones. Nowadays there are jugs made of high quality plastic that do not get scratched or discolored, but they are usually considerably more expensive. A blender does not have to be able to crush ice but it is definitely an advantage if it does.

If you are choosing between different machines, think about how often you want to make smoothies and how many. If you only make smoothies two or three times a month maybe the hand-held blender you already have in the kitchen drawer will be good enough, but if you want to become a smoothie freak, as I am, it is worth investing in a high quality machine that costs more, lasts longer, has a long guarantee, and can basically blend anything. A good blender pulverizes the ingredients thoroughly, which makes it easier for the body to absorb the nourishment. I use a *Vitamix* that can blend anything from seeds, nuts, ice, frozen fruit, and small berries to hard vegetables such as carrots, beets, and all kinds of leaves.

JUICER. To make smoothies with hard vegetables and fruit you need a juicer that first releases the juice. There are two kinds of juicer: a juice extractor and a juice press. When you are choosing your model, remember that performances differ and they produce different quantities of juice. If it is going to be used frequently it is probably better to invest in a proper press rather than in a juice extractor.

PRESS. Chops the fruit and vegetables into small pieces. These are then pressed through a fine metal sieve. Juice presses are slightly more expensive than juice extractors but can cope with bigger volumes and are more efficient. Also the juice is more nourishing since more enzymes are preserved in the process. Juice made with a press should be drunk within 48 hours, preferably immediately. The press should be washed up immediately after use to avoid the fruit residues getting dried and stuck on.

WHOLE FRUIT JUICER. Tears up the fruit and vegetables and whizzes the fruit flesh through a fine mesh. Whole fruit juicers are usually cheaper than presses but extract less juice. Also they destroy some of the enzymes as the rotating blades can get very hot. That also means that the juice oxidizes and has a somewhat shorter shelf-life. Juice made in a whole fruit juicer should be drunk within 24 hours, preferably immediately. It is important that the machine is washed up immediately after use, otherwise the fruit can get dried and stuck on.

CITRUS PRESS. You can go a long way with a simple manual citrus press. There are a lot of different variants, both electric and manual, and it is the quantity of juice that determines which model you need. If you are going to make one or two glasses of juice at a time it is easiest to use an ordinary manual citrus press; they are easy to clean, don't take up much room, and are relatively cheap. If you want to make bigger quantities of citrus juice it may be worth investing in a more sophisticated citrus press. Wash it up immediately after use to avoid the fruit residues drying and sticking on.

HAND BLENDER. A good choice if you don't make smoothies very often and then only in small quantities. The hand blender is easy to use and even easier to clean. But don't forget that it is designed to liquidize food, not to crush hard fruit or ice, and that the blades can snap if they are overloaded.

FOOD PROCESSOR. A good machine to have in the kitchen, but it is best suited to large quantities of smoothies or juices. Some of the contents of the smoothie tend to get stuck in the processor bowl since it is not very easy to empty. Often the food processor consists of lots of small parts and can therefore be difficult to clean.

USEFUL EQUIPMENT

ORANGE PEELER. Produces much thicker and longer strips of peel than a lemon grater and is much easier to peel with than an ordinary knife.

FRUIT BRUSH. Can be used instead of a peeler, since a lot of vitamins, antioxidants, fibers, and minerals are found in or just under the skin. Fruit brushes come in different hardnesses, so you need one for carrots, beets, and other hard root vegetables that need to be scrubbed thoroughly and a softer version for perishable fruit such as ripe pears and kiwifruit.

FREEZER. A big freezer is very useful if you are going to freeze large quantities of fruit, ice cubes, and smoothies. Fruit should not be stored for more than two to three months in a normal freezer, but may be stored a little longer if it is below 0 °F / −18 °C.

FREEZER BAGS. These are my best friends and irreplaceable when it comes to freezing fruit, herbs, and all sorts of other things. Freezer bags are space saving and hygienic. I usually buy masses of fruit when it is in season and freeze it in portions. Sealable bags that shut out the air effectively are best. Don't forget to put a label on them showing the contents, date, number of portions, and if appropriate the weight. Freezer bags and self-adhesive labels are available from any large local supermarket.

ICE CREAM MOLDS. Perfect for turning your smoothie or fruit juice into refreshing ice pops. Enjoyed by both adults and children and much better for you than readymade mixes. Remember not to use ice in these smoothies and to make the flavor a little more concentrated than usual.

ICE MOLDS. Really essential, for example when you want to freeze coconut water, coconut milk, passion fruit, fruit purée, freshly squeezed juice, or left-over smoothie or liquid bases, such as oat, soy, or nut milk. I freeze everything that is left over or can be used for a chilled smoothie. The cubes act as both flavoring and stabilizers, and take the place of ordinary ice. Transfer them to a plastic bag as soon as they have frozen and seal it carefully, then they will keep for a long time in the freezer.

CRUSHED ICE. Not necessary if your blender can cope with blending whole pieces of ice. You can also crush ice by hand by wrapping the ice cubes in a clean dish towel and banging them with a heavy object such as a hammer.

KNIVES, BIG AND SMALL. High quality stainless steel knives are best. Always use big knives (preferably slightly flexible ones) for big fruit so that you get whole slices and don't lose any of your fingers. With small knives you can make decorations from both peel and whole fruit. The sharper and thinner the knife, the easier it is to fillet grapefruit, oranges, and other citrus fruit or peel some fruit really finely, such as kiwifruit. Since many of the vitamins lie in or just under the skin, the less fruit you cut off, the better.

REFRIGERATOR. All dairy products, freshly squeezed juices, and open packs of nut milk must be stored in the fridge, likewise most fruit. To make sure they do not become overripe or become contaminated by other foods, it is best to keep fruit in sealed plastic bags. On the other hand, if you want the fruit to ripen it should be stored at room temperature instead.

KITCHEN SCALES. These are good for measuring precise proportions of all the ingredients. They can also be used when you want to freeze fruit in exactly the right size portions. In the recipes I give the weight of fruit and nuts, and also the volume in cups, but the volume can vary. You can also use your eyes and sense of taste to determine the amounts. Fruit often varies in flavor depending on the season and variety, so small differences in weight do not matter much when you are making smoothies, unless you are counting calories. The important thing is that you like the taste and that you learn to experiment.

SET OF MEASURING CUPS. These are useful tools for measuring out juice, nut milk, yogurt, spices, and other ingredients. If you are experienced your eyes should tell you a lot.

OLIVE PITTER. These make life a lot easier—if you want to pit cherries or other small fruit for instance. Of course you can also use a very pointed small knife, but an olive pitter does the job much more easily and quickly.

POTATO PEELER. This is an essential utensil in the kitchen for peeling mangos, hard root vegetables, and nonorganically grown fruit such as apples and pears. Organic and locally produced fruit and vegetables do not usually need peeling, but if you are not sure you can wash and peel them as thinly as possible. Waxed and sprayed fruit should always be peeled, otherwise there is a risk that you will absorb toxins that are bad for your body. There are special fruit washing products that dissolve the wax and other spray pesticides.

GRATER. Very useful for grating lemon peel, ginger, carrots, beets, and other things before they go in the blender or are used for decoration. A stainless steel grater is best for acid and citrus fruit.

SIEVE. Press the smoothie through a fine sieve to filter out pieces of peel and pits. I sieve orange, lemon, and lime juice also, to get rid of the taste of the bitter pits. It is a good idea to use a plastic sieve for acid fruit as metal can affect the taste.

CHOPPING BOARD. Always keep a separate chopping board for fruit and vegetables. Remember to wash it immediately after use, otherwise it can become discolored and absorb flavors. Even with careful cleaning it can be a breeding ground for bacteria, so replace it as soon as it gets scratched or discolored.

SPATULA. This is a useful tool for scraping out the blender so that none of the good stuff is wasted.

APPLE CORER. This makes life easier if you can't be bothered to cut and core the apples and pears with an ordinary knife—what's more, you get whole fruit rings that can be used for decoration.

TIPS AND ADVICE

BOOST THE NUTRITIONAL CONTENT

There are lots of nutritious things you can boost your smoothie with. It is easy to supplement the nutritional content and adjust the recipe to just what your body needs. Most of these added ingredients can be found in health food shops, and many of them are also available in well-stocked supermarkets in general.

One kind of extra nutritious supplement is dried super fruit and powdered berries such as acai, goji, lucuma, rose hips, inca berries, mulberries, maqui, buckthorn, cranberries, and blueberries. Healthy cold pressed oils such as linseed oil, coconut oil, and hempseed oil are brilliant for providing the body with an extra energy boost, too. Or why not add a little extra fiber with, for instance, linseed, chia seeds, hemp seeds, oat germ, or wheatgerm? You can also mix in various powdered seaweeds, such as spirulina, chlorella, arame, wakame, and dulse, or superfood powders such as maca, corn grass, nettle powder, and wheatgrass.

If you want to boost the smoothie with extra proteins, there are various wholly natural, vegan, and GM-free protein powders in different flavors. You can also try raw brown rice protein, pea protein, hemp protein, oat protein, and seaweed protein. And don't forget all the nutritious nuts, seeds, nut oils, and nut butters that are also great for blending into smoothies.

TONING DOWN THE FLAVOR

Some fruit and vegetables have very strong flavors and need to be used in small quantities. For example if you have too much chili or ginger in your smoothie it will become undrinkable. Taste it while you are making it and dilute it with bland juices if it is too strong. If you think one flavor is too dominant, add a little water and juice from, for instance, carrots, apples, pears, or oranges.

ENHANCING THE FLAVOR

Some fruit, such as melon, mango, and banana, are particularly sweet and can make the smoothie nauseating. A useful trick for reducing the sweetness is to add a little lemon or lime juice, which also enhances the fruitiness.

THINNER SMOOTHIES

If the smoothie is too thick and the consistency is like a purée—which can happen if the fruit does not contain much liquid—you can thin it with a little water, nut milk, or freshly pressed juice. In order to preserve the pure fruit taste, water is the best option.

THICKER SMOOTHIES

If the smoothie is too thin you can try adding a little soy yogurt, banana, avocado, mango, or protein powder. You can also add tofu, muesli, nuts, or other healthy ingredients that will absorb a little of the liquid.

SMOOTHER SMOOTHIES

Some fruit and vegetables are very rich in fiber, and they will make the smoothie coarse and difficult to drink if the blender does not pulverize them properly. In that situation you can run them through a juicer first (or blend them into a purée) and then press the fruit juice through a fine sieve before mixing it all with the other ingredients.

CHILLED SMOOTHIES

If you want to make a refreshing and icy smoothie, the best way is to use frozen fruit. It also works if you blend ice into the finished smoothie. Remember that the ice will melt if the smoothie is too warm, so it is a good idea to refrigerate the fruit before preparing the smoothie. It is better to use too much ice than too little, small quantities melt quickly and make the smoothie watery.

POPSICLES MADE FROM SMOOTHIES

Most fruit smoothies can be made into popsicles. Leave out the ice and most of the water from your recipe and try to make the flavor a little more concentrated—ice cream has less flavor because it is so cold. Pour the smoothie into ice cream molds with a stick in the middle and place them in the freezer. You can make the ice cream stripy by filling the mold with smoothies of various colors and flavors; allow each layer to freeze for 30–45 minutes before you add the next so that they do not run together. Do not fill the molds up to the edge as the liquid expands slightly in the freezer. The popsicles keep for a week in the freezer, after that they become icy and lose their flavor.

SERVE IMMEDIATELY

To do justice to the vitamins, flavor, color, and consistency you should serve smoothies and freshly pressed juices as soon as possible after preparing them. Home-made smoothies do not contain any preservatives and are not pasteurized either. If you want to save your smoothie for later, it can be stored in a clean, sealed glass container in the refrigerator but preferably not for more than 24 hours, as the vitamins disappear slowly but surely and it will go off quite quickly. Shake the smoothie well before you drink it if it has been standing in the refrigerator for a while.

DECORATION

Don't forget to decorate your smoothies. Serve them in attractive glasses and decorate them with fresh fruit, herbs, edible flowers, and other pretty things. You can buy fun ice molds, cocktail stirrers, umbrellas, and similar things in craft shops, or you can make them yourself or bring them home from your holidays.

CREATE YOUR OWN RECIPES

Be creative and invent your own recipes. You can really use whatever ingredients you like in a smoothie. Your imagination is the only limit, so experiment!

INGREDIENTS

A GUIDE TO FRUIT AND VEGETABLES

APPLE. Contains a lot of vitamin C, antioxidants, and dietary fiber. Apples should be stored cool, prefer- ably in a plastic bag in the refrigerator, since they do not keep long at room temperature. They give off ethylene gas, which accelerates their ripening. Freshly picked apples are by far the most delicious. Freshly pressed juice freezes well as ice cubes.

APRICOT. Looks like a plum but is yellowish orange and the skin is slightly downy. Apricots contain beta-carotene, which is converted to vitamin A in the body. There is also a lot of dietary fiber, vitamin C, potassium, calcium, magnesium, and vitamin B6 in apricots. The fruit can be kept at room temperature for one to two days, but is best kept in the refrigerator.

AVOCADO. Contains vitamin E among other things. An avocado is ripe when the flesh feels a little springy and gives a little when you press the top slightly. To find a perfect avocado you should buy it hard and keep it at room temperature for three to four days. It will ripen and become softer. Ripening can be accelerated if you place the avocado in a paper or plastic bag with apples, pears, or bananas. A ripe avocado can be kept for about three days in a plastic bag in the vegetable drawer of the refrigerator. If you keep it too cold it will not ripen and the flesh will turn brown.

BANANA. These are green and unripe when they are imported and then ripen with the help of ethylene gas (see page 13). Bananas contain a lot of potassium, vitamin B6, and magnesium. They should be kept at room temperature or in a cool place—preferably in a separate bowl slightly apart from other fruit. Keeping them too cold can make bananas go black. Bananas are sensitive to impact; if they are squeezed they go brown quickly and the flesh is damaged. Bananas are particularly good for freezing and give a lot of smoothies a creamy sweet flavor. Choose ripe bananas, peel them, and cut them into smaller pieces. Freeze the pieces on a tray first and then transfer them to a freezer bag which can be sealed. I usually cut a banana into five pieces.

BEETS. Contain large quantities of potassium, iron, folic acid, calcium, magnesium, phosphorus, manga- nese, and vitamin C. In addition the leaves contain the antioxidant beta-carotene. There are yellow beets and attractive-looking spotted beets, which look like beets on the outside but are stripy on the inside. For the best shelf-life, store beets in a plastic bag in the refrigerator. At 40 °F / 4 °C they will last about six months but at room temperature only ten days. Freshly pressed juice works well if frozen as ice cubes.

BLACKBERRIES. A good source of vitamin C, vitamin E, vitamin K, potassium, manganese, magnesium, iron, and fiber. To find tasty, wild blackberries it is important to wait until the berries are really ripe. Cultivated blackberries can be picked earlier. Blackberries keep for one day at room temperature, but they freeze well. The berries are sensitive, so one tip is to pick them directly into a plastic bag and freeze them immediately.

BLUEBERRIES. Contain high levels of vitamin C and vitamin B, and a lot of antioxidants. If you pick them in the woods, remember to pick only the blue berries, not the black ones. If you buy them in a shop, try to find even size, plump fruit that is not wrinkly. The shelf-life of blueberries in the refrigerator is 24–48 hours, but they freeze well. In shops you can buy blueberries from different countries. Some are a little bigger than others. These have a fruitier flavor and keep very well in a cool place. However they do not contain such large quantities of antioxidants as the smaller ones.

BROCCOLI. For vegans and others who do not eat dairy products, broccoli is a valuable source of calcium. There is plenty of vitamin C in broccoli, but it also contains other important vitamins, including vitamins A, B9 (folic acid), and K, and also fiber. Broccoli also contains some vitamin E, iron, calcium, potassium, magnesium, zinc, and vitamins B1, B2, B3, and B6. Broccoli is best stored in a plastic bag in the vegetable drawer of the refrigerator.

BUCKTHORN. The yellow berries of the buckthorn contain large quantities of vitamin C and also B12, which is rare in the plant world and particularly important for vegetarians. They also contain vitamins B1, B2, B3 (niacin), B6, B9 (folic acid), pantothenic acid, biotin, vitamin E, and vitamin K. Buckthorn berries keep in the refrigerator for a week. Whole buckthorn berries can be frozen, as can buckthorn juice, which can be frozen as cubes.

CAPE GOOSEBERRY / PHYSALIS. Contains a lot of vitamins A and C. The fruit is enclosed in a brown, papery case which is not edible. However you can eat the whole of the yellowish orange fruit—skin and all. It is not related to the gooseberry but belongs to the same family as the potato. If you keep them in their papery cases physalis will last a couple of weeks in the refrigerator. The fruit can also be frozen, if so remove the case.

CARROT. Arrived in Europe from Central Asia in the twelfth century, but at that time it was bright red in color. Carrots contain beta-carotene, which is converted to vitamin A in the body. It is carotene that gives carrots their orange color. Carrots are best stored without their leaves in a plastic bag in the refrigerator or a cool place. The leaves of carrots should be cut off since they steal nourishment and make the carrots go soft. Freshly pressed juice freezes well as ice cubes.

CELERY. Celery has high levels of potassium and is an excellent source of vitamins C and A, calcium, and protein. The green leaves should be used within two days, otherwise they may shrivel and the levels of vitamin C, calcium, and potassium will drop. When you buy celery, look for straight, firm stalks that snap if you bend them and leaves that have not begun to turn yellow or wilt. Store the celery in the refrigerator in a sealed container or wrapped in a plastic bag or damp cloth. Celery should not be stored at room temperature for long as its high water content means that it wilts quickly. If it starts to droop, splash it with water and put it in the refrigerator to restore its crispness.

CHERRIES including BIGARREAU. There are sweet cherries and sour cherries. Bigarreau cherries are sweet cherries rich in vitamin C. Cherries contain potassium and dietary fiber and some research has suggested that they have anti-inflammatory effects. Look for plump, firm fruit that have no blemishes, are shiny, and have good stalks. Cherries keep for two days at room temperature and up to a couple of weeks in the refrigerator. They are sensitive to pressure and do not do well if they are packed in a bag. Cherries freeze well, but take the pits out first.

CITRUS FRUIT. This is the collective name for a large number of fruit rich in vitamin C, among others oranges, clementines, lemons, grapefruit, limes, mandarins, and satsumas. All citrus fruit can be stored at room temperature and in the refrigerator. Citrus fruit with thin peel are juicier if they are kept at room temperature, while the thicker skinned ones produce more fruit juice if they are kept cold. Freshly pressed citrus juice can be frozen like ice cubes.

CLEMENTINES, SATSUMAS, and MANDARINS. All three are small citrus fruit. Mandarins have a lot of pits and that is why they are not imported much. Clementines and satsumas are easy to peel and almost always seedless. Satsuma peel may be somewhat green even though, like all other citrus fruit, it is harvested ripe.

CRANBERRIES. Grown on marshland, and have also been called marsh berries. Cranberries contain a lot of vitamin C and antioxidants and are good for infections of the urinary tract and caries, among other things. When cranberries have felt the first frost the flavor is somewhat sweeter but they can also be picked earlier in the year, in which case they need to be frozen before they are used.

CUCUMBER. Contains some vitamin C and vitamin K. Our most water-rich vegetable should be firm and not bend at all, if it does it is beginning to go off. Cucumbers keep best in a plastic bag in the refrigerator or at 45–55 °F / 7–14 °C. At room temperature cucumbers soon curl but they are also sensitive to cold. Plastic-wrapped cucumber should be kept in the plastic to protect it against drying out, getting bruised, and exposure to ethylene gas from other vegetables that can accelerate ripening.

DATES. These are so-called drupes. Dates grow to about 1½ inches / 4 cm long and contain a lot of dietary fiber, together with potassium, vitamin A, and vitamin D. Dates do not suffer from drying out and can keep for up to two months if they are stored at freezing point. They can also be thawed and refrozen.

GRAPEFRUIT. If you eat half a grapefruit daily you obtain more vitamin C than you need each day. The taste is aromatic and fresh but also a little bitter owing to the small quantities of quinine it contains. Choose a fruit that is firm and undamaged. Its shelf-life varies depending on what country it has come from. Grapefruit keep best if they are stored in a cool place at 50–75 °F / 10–15 °C. People with cardiovascular problems should be careful with grapefruit because it can alter the effects of some medicines. Freshly pressed juice can be frozen as ice cubes.

GRAPES. Contain vitamin C, potassium, and a lot of dietary fiber. Grapes are always harvested ripe and have a short shelf-life. They should be eaten immediately or stored in a plastic bag in the refrigerator, where they can keep for a week. They taste best if they are allowed to stand for 20 minutes at room temperature before they are used.

KIWIFRUIT. Rich in vitamin C and potassium. Kiwifruit can be eaten with or without the skin. Green flesh is commonest but kiwifruit with yellow flesh also exist, and have a slightly sweeter flavor. Kiwifruit ripen in a few days at room temperature. Ripening can be accelerated if you place the fruit in a plastic bag together with an apple. Unripe kiwifruit keep for up to three weeks in a plastic bag in the refrigerator. Throw away fruit that is wrinkled or mushy. The national symbol of New Zealand, the kiwi bird, gives the fruit its name.

LIME. Rich in vitamin C. A relative of lemons and used in the same way, but they have a somewhat more rounded and aromatic flavor. It is a good idea to keep limes in the chiller section of the refrigerator since they are not frost resistant. Freshly pressed juice can be frozen as ice cubes.

LINGON BERRIES. Contain moderate quantities of potassium, calcium, iron, phosphorus, vitamin A, vitamin C, and vitamin E. Lingon berries are fine in the refrigerator, in a plastic box lined with kitchen paper. They will keep for a couple of weeks like that, sometimes even up to a month. Lingon berries contain benzoic acid that extends their shelf-life and means that uncooked lingon jam with small quantities of sugar in it can be kept without preservatives. The fresh fruit also freezes well.

MANGO. Mangos are particularly rich in beta-carotene, which is converted to vitamin A in the body and also contain plenty of vitamin C and potassium. Mangos, like cashew nuts, contain the substance urushiol and those with allergies should be careful, at least when handling the skin.

Squeeze the fruit to choose one that is ripe. It should give a little under pressure but should not be too soft. You can also sniff it and notice how it smells. On the other hand, you cannot tell from the skin color whether it is ripe, since there are over a thousand known varieties of mango in various colors. Mangos keep for up to two weeks in the refrigerator. At room temperature they ripen quickly in a bag with apples or bananas. When they have ripened mangos can be kept in the refrigerator for a few days, but no cooler than 50 °F / 10 °C. If they are peeled and diced they keep well in freezer bags, but cut out the pit first.

MELON. Related to pumpkins and cucumbers. There is a difference between sweet melon and water-melon. The seeds of the sweet melon are bunched together in the middle, while those of the watermelon are in the flesh of the melon (read more under watermelon). Sniff the melon when you are buying one. If you can smell it at the flowering end (opposite where the stalk was) it is ripe. Store the melon at room temperature if it is whole. If you have started cutting into it, it should be kept in the refrigerator. Melons give off ethylene gas, which accelerates ripening.

NECTARINE. Contains vitamins A, B, and C. It is a kind of peach with a smooth skin. It often has a more intense flavor than the peach. Unripe nectarines ripen at room temperature, ripe ones can be kept in a plastic bag in the refrigerator. At room temperature the shelf-life of ripe nectarines is one to two days. Nectarines give off a lot of ethylene gas and have a short shelf-life.

ORANGE. All citrus fruit are rich in vitamin C. Be careful with the big specimens. They often have a rather insipid flavor. Instead look for oranges that are heavy for their size and especially those that have a smooth, thin skin. Oranges are best stored in a plastic bag in the refrigerator, but they can last for one to two weeks at room temperature. Freshly pressed orange juice can be frozen like ice cubes and then trans-ferred to sealable freezer bags so that they do not come into contact with the air or with other flavors.

PAPAYA. Papaya is rich in vitamins A, C, E, and B, plus antioxidants such as carotene, zeaxanthin, and flavonoids. Several important minerals, such as potassium, magnesium, calcium, and iron, are also found in papaya, together with the enzyme papain, which is used as a remedy for digestive problems. Papaya keeps up to three weeks in the refrigerator. An unripe fruit ripens in a couple of days at room temperature. Papaya has an inedible yellowish green skin and orange flesh that is sweet and delicious. When the fruit is ripe it should have an even color. To enhance the flavor you can squeeze a little lime juice over the flesh. People do not usually eat the seeds of the papaya even though they are edible. They taste a little peppery and are not suitable for mixing into smoothies or juices. Papayas freeze well if you peel them first, remove the seeds, and cut them into pieces.

PASSION FRUIT. Contains vitamin C, carotene, potassium, and dietary fiber. The commonest passion fruit is the reddish-mauve variety, but there are also slightly larger reddish-yellow and yellow varieties. Passion fruit contains potassium and beta-carotene among other things. When you buy passion fruit it should be firm and a little wrinkled—but not too wrinkled, which would mean it is old. It should not be too light either because then it might be dry inside. In the refrigerator it keeps for three to four weeks. The flesh of the passion fruit freezes well as ice cubes, stored in sealable freezer bags. The cubes keep for two to three months in the freezer.

PEACH. Contains vitamins A, B, and C. It ripens quickly at room temperature and can only be left out for one or two days. In the refrigerator it can be kept for up to two weeks. It is best to store it in a plastic bag to prevent its drying out. Nectarines are a kind of peach with a smooth skin. They often have a more intense flavor than peaches.

PEAR. Has been grown for several thousand years. In addition to dietary fiber pears are rich in potassium, riboflavin, and vitamins A and C. Pears have a short shelf-life and are best stored in a plastic bag in the refrigerator, but they should be left out at room temperature for four to six days before being eaten so they develop as much flavor as possible. Pears give off ethylene gas, which accelerates ripening when with other fruit in the fruit bowl.

PEAS. Green peas are rich in vitamin B9 (folic acid), and also contain vitamins C, B1, B2, B3, and B6, iron, magnesium, potassium, zinc, and a lot of dietary fiber. Peas are easiest to buy frozen.

PINEAPPLE. Contains a lot of vitamin C and dietary fiber. To check whether a pineapple is ripe, you can try pulling off one of the outer leaves. If it comes off easily the fruit is ripe. The safest way is to buy an unripe pineapple and let it ripen at home. In the refrigerator a ripe pineapple will keep for up to a week, at room temperature for up to about three days. Pineapple works well if you freeze it in pieces—cut it through the middle, take out the hard center, and then cut up the flesh.

PLUM. Rich in vitamins A, C, E, B2, B3, and B6, and in calcium, iron, magnesium, phosphorus, and dietary fiber. Plums are drupes and they come in various colors and sizes. Dried plums are called prunes and are also very nutritious. Unripe plums ripen in a few days at room temperature. Ripe plums are best stored cool in the refrigerator.

POMEGRANATE. Contains a lot of folic acid and antioxidants, together with vitamin C, carotene, gallo-catechins, and anthocyanins (which give the pomegranate its pink color). People eat the sweet–sour seeds and the jelly-like flesh round them. The strong color of the seeds is sometimes used to color drinks and is then called *grenadine*. Ripe pomegranates are brownish-red, but since they do not keep very well it is better to choose a red one that has not had time to ripen fully. If the skin is hard and dry the fruit has been stored for too long. In the refrigerator a pomegranate will keep for about two weeks. Press and freeze the pomegranate juice as ice cubes and store them in a sealable freezer bag. The cubes can be stored for two to three months in the freezer and used in any smoothie you like. Pomegranate seeds also freeze well.

RASPBERRIES. Most raspberries are red, but black and yellow varieties also exist. Raspberries contain vitamin C and dietary fiber among other things. The berries should be evenly colored and should not be kept for more than two days. Raspberries freeze well and will then keep for two to three months.

REDCURRANTS and BLACKCURRANTS. There are black, red, yellow, and white currants. Regardless of their color they contain plenty of vitamins A, C, and K, potassium, and masses of dietary fiber. The seeds of the blackcurrant also contain gamma-linolenic acid, vitamin E, and important polyunsaturated fatty acids which have been shown to have a cholesterol-reducing effect, among other things. The optimum health-giving effect from blackcurrants is obtained when the seeds are crushed, as in blackcurrant powder. At room temperature currants keep for two to three days, in the refrigerator for about a week. Currants freeze very well.

RHUBARB. Rich in vitamin C and iron. Rhubarb freezes well. At room temperature rhubarb quickly becomes limp but the stalks can be stored for a week in the refrigerator, wrapped in plastic film.

SPINACH. A super food with a lot of antioxidants. Spinach is incredibly nutritious and contains vitamins A, B9 (folic acid), C, E, and K among others, copper, iron, magnesium, calcium, chlorophyll, and fiber. Fresh spinach keeps for about a week in the refrigerator in an air-filled plastic bag.

STRAWBERRIES. They contain more vitamin C than oranges and they are also fairly rich in iron. Be careful when choosing strawberries and make sure they are not overripe or mushy. Strawberries are very sensitive to handling and go off if they are too tightly packed. They can be kept in the refrigerator for a little while but are definitely at their best on the day of purchase. If you are freezing them either cut them up or freeze them whole, but take the stalks off first. In the freezer they keep for two to three months, like most soft fruit.

WATERMELON. Contains vitamins A, B, and C. The commonest watermelon has a green skin but there are also varieties with spotted green and yellow skins. Watermelon works very well in smoothies because it contains a lot of water. Choose a firm melon and tap it. If it sounds hollow it is ripe. Whole watermelons keep for up to 12 days at room temperature, depending on the variety and degree of ripeness, and even longer in the refrigerator.

FROZEN FRUIT AND BERRY FRUIT
Nowadays you can buy frozen fruit all year round. At the freezer counter you can also find frozen packs with individual portions of smoothie mixes that are ready for blending. Provided the fruit has been frozen immediately after harvesting this is an excellent alternative if there is no fresh produce in the shop.

It is a good idea to freeze fruit yourself when it is in season, then you know where it has come from and that it is of good quality. What is more, it is usually both tastier and more economical to buy fruit when it is in season. Read more about how to freeze fruit on page 12.

DRIED FRUIT
A lot of fruit can be bought dried. Like frozen produce, this is a good alternative when the fruit is not in season. Make sure that it does not contain sugar, oil, flavorings, colorants, or preservatives. If possible choose organic fruit because that is guaranteed to be free from toxic pesticides. You can tell good produce by the fact that the list of ingredients does not include anything except the fruit itself.

Soak the dried fruit for a little while before you use it. The bigger the fruit, the longer it takes to soften. Just remember not to pour hot or, even worse, boiling water on it since if you do a lot of the nutrients will disappear. I always recommend washing dried fruit before you use it if it does not expressly state that it has been washed before drying.

PRESERVED FRUIT
I prefer not to use preserved fruit in my smoothies but, if you do, remember to choose fruit that is not preserved in syrup and does not contain colorants, flavorings, or additives. It should preferably be in its own juice.

BERRY POWDER
If you cannot get hold of fresh berry fruit, berry powder is a good alternative. It is made of whole, freeze-dried fruit that have been ground to a powder, including the fruit flesh, peel, and seeds. Among others acai, lucuma, maqui berries, buckthorn, blueberries, pomegranate, raspberry, strawberry, rose hip, and cranberry powders are available. Berry powder is very practical since it lasts for up to 18 months. You can add the powder directly to the smoothie, but don't forget that berry powders are quite concentrated. There are a lot of different kinds on sale in health food shops. If possible choose organic ones.

GIVE YOUR SMOOTHIE A BOOST

SUPERFOODS AND SUPER BERRIES

ACAI BERRIES. These are super berries from the rainforests of South America and they are stuffed with antioxidants, vitamins, and essential fats. They have high levels of vitamins B and C, minerals, fiber, and protein. Since the berries become stale very quickly, they are usually sold as pasteurized juice. In the pasteurization process unfortunately a lot of the nutritional content is lost, and therefore freeze-dried acai berries are a better alternative. The powder is on sale in well-stocked health food shops.

CAMU CAMU BERRIES. One of the richest berries for vitamin C that there is. They contain up to 60 times as much antioxidant vitamin C as oranges. The berries also contain the B vitamins niacin, thiamine, and riboflavin as well as the minerals iron, phosphorus, potassium, and calcium. Camu camu is a health "bomb" that protects against free radicals and can help prevent cancer, diabetes, neurological diseases, and premature aging. Organic camu camu powder is made from deseeded dried berries that have been carefully ground at low temperatures—in order to preserve the nutrients of the berries in the best way possible. The recommended daily dose is half to one teaspoon.

COCOA NIBS, RAW. These are 100 percent raw, lightly roasted, and crushed cocoa beans. Contain over three hundred nutritious substances, among others high levels of antioxidants, magnesium, iron, chromium, and vitamin C, plus serotonin—which makes us happy and contented. The fact that the cocoa is *raw* means that it has been roasted at below 105 °F / 40 °C in order to preserve the healthy nutrients. Does not contain sugar, dairy products, or additives. Store in an airtight container in a dark and cool place. Can be kept for a couple of years.

CORN GRASS. Stuffed full of vitamins, minerals, amino acids, antioxidants, dietary fiber, and chlorophyll. Corn grass contains 11 times more calcium and 30 times more vitamin B1 than cow's milk, 5 times more iron than spinach, 7 times more vitamin C than oranges, and 25 times more potassium than bananas. It also contains significant quantities of vitamin B12 and 18 different amino acids. Mix corn grass in with your favorite smoothie and drink it on an empty stomach; that way the nourishment will be absorbed more quickly. Store the powder in a dry, cool place away from direct sunlight. The recommended daily dose is one teaspoon. Corn grass powder is sold in health food shops.

GOJI BERRIES. A super berry that has a strong effect on the immune system and contains 18 different amino acids, of which 7 are vital. The berries also contain important minerals, such as iron, calcium, zinc, selenium, copper, calcium, germanium, and phosphorus, plus vitamins B1, B2, B6, and E. It tastes like a cross between lingon berries and raisins. The recommended daily dose is roughly a small handful / 20–30 grams of whole berries or one teaspoon of berry powder. Store in a dry, dark, and cool place in a sealed pack, avoiding direct sunlight. An opened pack of dried goji berries should be consumed within two months.

INCA. A relation of physalis, containing as much as 16 percent protein. Inca berries are very nutritious and contain, among other things, bioflavonoids that boost the uptake of vitamin C by cells. Inca berries also contain phosphorus, vitamins A, C, B1, B2, B6, and B12, plus a lot of carotenoids and pectin. Pectin is good for the digestion among other things, and for lowering cholesterol levels. The dried berries are sold in well-stocked health food shops.

LUCUMA, POWDER. Lucuma is a nutritious fruit that tastes of toffee. It is rich in fiber, antioxidants, vitamins, and minerals—especially vitamins C and B, beta-carotene, calcium, phosphorus, and iron. In lucuma powder all the nutrients of the fruit are preserved in a concentrated form. The powder is sold in well-stocked health food shops.

MACA ROOT, POWDER. Contains large quantities of amino acids, carbohydrates, and minerals such as calcium, zinc, magnesium, and iron. The maca root also contains vitamins B1, B2, B12, C, and E. Since the taste of maca powder is very distinct and can take over (it is somewhat reminiscent of horseradish), it is best to take a little at a time and taste as you go. It is a good idea to mix it with other strong flavors. Available as a powder in health food shops.

MAQUI BERRIES. Contain four times as many antioxidants as blueberries and twice as many as acai berries. That makes maqui an effective weapon against free radicals. What is more, the berries protect the body's cells against oxidative stress and counteract premature aging. Maqui berries are filled to the brim with flavonoids, polyphenols, and vitamins A, C, and E, plus the minerals calcium, potassium, and iron. Freeze-dried berry powder is sold in well-stocked health food shops.

MULBERRIES. Contain a lot of vitamin C, vitamin K, iron, and calcium. Mulberries are also a good source of resveratrol, an antioxidant and anticoagulant substance with a range of health-giving effects. Dried mulberries can be found in most well-stocked food stores and health food shops. It is best to buy the organic berries. The recommended daily dose is roughly a small handful / 20–30 grams.

ROSE HIP POWDER, WHOLE. Made from the whole rose hip—in other words the skin, flesh, and seeds. Contains 60 times more vitamin C than citrus fruit and is rich in antioxidants and vital minerals such as iron, calcium, potassium, and magnesium. A tablespoon of whole rose hip powder is equivalent to a whole bowl of fresh rose hips. The recommended daily dose is one to three tablespoons in cold water or food. The powder should not be heated to more than 105 °F / 40 °C because that reduces the effect of the antioxidants. Do not confuse whole rose hip powder with ordinary rose hip powder that contains only the outer layer of the rose hip plus additives and sugar. Whole rose hip powder should be stored in a dry, cool place in a sealed pack. That way it will keep for about two years. People who are taking blood-thinning medication should consult their doctor before they consume whole rose hip powder.

STINGING NETTLE. Contains a lot of chlorophyll and also provitamin A, beta-carotene, calcium, potassium, magnesium, iron, silicon, manganese, flavonoids, vitamins C, B, and K, plus folic acid. When the plant is dried or cooked the stinging effect disappears. Pick young shoots and dry, blanch, or freeze them. Also available in powdered form. Dried nettles should be stored away from the light in a sealed pack. Can be stored for about two years.

WHEAT GRASS. This is almost a complete food and contains over 20 amino acids, several hundred enzymes, 90 minerals, and a whole lot of vitamins. About 70 percent of the content of wheat grass is chlorophyll, the basis of plant life and also good for people. Mix it in with your favorite smoothie and drink it on an empty stomach; that way the nourishment will be absorbed more quickly. Store in a dry, cool place away from direct sunlight. The recommended daily dose is one teaspoon. Wheat grass powder is sold in health food shops.

SWEETENERS

I only use natural sweeteners such as coconut sugar, agave syrup, stevia, lucuma powder, mesquite powder, dates, dried fruits, and sweet fruits to sweeten my smoothies. Since I never use artificial sweeteners myself I cannot give any recommendations for them either.

NUT BUTTER

Nut butter has become popular among health conscious consumers for its high fiber content, protein, healthy fats, minerals, vitamins, and antioxidants. In addition it has a satiating effect. A good nut butter should be organically produced and consist of at least 99 percent nuts. It should not contain anything other than, possibly, a little sea salt. However for smoothies unsalted nut butter works best. There are a lot of different kinds of nut butters to choose from. Unfortunately some of them contain both palm oil and sugar—beware of those! Blend the nut butter directly into the smoothie or mix it with water first to make nut milk. Nut butter is sold in health food shops and well-stocked supermarkets.

SEAWEED

Seaweed is a very good source of protein. The body can take up four times more protein from the blue-green seaweed spirulina than from meat. Spirulina is sometimes cited as the seaweed that could be the answer to world hunger. It contains so many nutrients that NASA usually includes it in the provisions for their astronauts. Other healthy seaweeds are chlorella, arame, wakame, and dulse.

CHLORELLA. This is a single-cell green seaweed that has flourished on earth for several hundred millions of years. It contains about 60 percent protein and a large number of valuable amino acids. This seaweed also contains important vitamins and minerals, such as vitamins A, C, and E, several B-vitamins, iron, calcium, and magnesium. It is rich in chlorophyll, which helps to boost the immune system and cleanse the blood. Chlorella is believed to clear the body of heavy metals and other toxins, aid digestion, and neutralize the body's pH—which is often far too acid.

SPIRULINA. This is an extremely nutritious seaweed that contains a lot of protein and also important minerals, vitamins, fatty acids, and antioxidants. Spirulina is believed among other things to strengthen the immune system, prevent harmful bacterial and viral growth, and have a protective effect against cancer. Spirulina can also boost the memory and learning capacity and prevent and alleviate hay fever. The recommended daily dose is one teaspoon. Spirulina should be stored in a dry, cool place.

PROTEIN POWDER

Examples of vegan protein powders are raw brown rice protein, pea protein, hemp protein, oat protein, tempeh, miso, ground nuts, soymilk, and seaweed. Spirulina for example contains up to 65 percent protein. Ask in your health food shop for more information and advice.

HEALTHY OILS

It is fine to use cold pressed healthy oils in your smoothies. Examples are coconut oil, linseed oil, and hempseed oil. Ask in your health food shop for more information and advice.

COCONUT OIL. This is one of the world's healthiest oils. It is solid at room temperature but becomes liquid at around 75 °F / 24 °C. About 50 percent of the fat consists of lauric acid that the body converts to mono-lauric acid, which inhibits viruses, fungi, and bacteria. Coconut oil is good for food preparation, smoothies, and desserts, and for skincare. Always choose organic, raw, cold pressed, unbleached, unrefined, and undeodorized coconut oil. The list of ingredients should say 100 percent coconut. Store away from light in a cool place. It is sold in supermarkets and health food shops.

HEMP SEED OIL. Produced by pressing hempseed. Hempseed oil is considered to be one of nature's most valuable vegetable oils because it contains the highest proportion of polyunsaturated fatty acids. Cold pressed organic hempseed oil is an excellent food for vegetarians and vegans because it ensures a balanced protein intake. The oil also contains quite a lot of omega-3, omega-6, and omega-9, which are otherwise obtained from fish. An opened bottle should be stored in the refrigerator and used within four weeks. Sold in health food shops.

LINSEED OIL. Produced from cold pressed linseeds, depending on the manufacturer it contains 50–65 percent omega-3. The contents include among other things omega-6, omega-9, and vitamin E. The oil should ideally be organic and cold pressed. The recommended daily dose is one to two teaspoons. An opened bottle should be kept in the refrigerator and used within four weeks. Sold in health food shops.

NUTRITIOUS FLAVORINGS

CARDAMOM. Contains a lot of antioxidants that boost the immune system. Cardamom is soothing and diuretic, good for the digestion, and helps keep blood pressure down.

CINNAMON. Manufactured from the bark of the cinnamon tree, it contains a number of healthy antioxidants, and is said to be equivalent to five hundred times its weight in fresh tomatoes. It is a super spice with a number of healthy effects, among others a beneficial effect on the intestinal flora. Cinnamon also helps to keep the blood sugar level even and is thought to reduce the risk of type 2 diabetes and heart disease.

COCOA POWDER. Contains over three hundred nutritious substances, including high levels of antioxidants, magnesium, iron, chromium, vitamin C, and endorphins. The powder is made by cold pressing cocoa beans and straining off the cocoa butter. The temperature has to be carefully monitored and reach no more than 105 °F / 40 °C so that none of the nutrients is lost. The dry cake is then ground and filtered to make a fine powder. Cocoa powder is easy to mix with other ingredients and is fully absorbed by the body.

Do not mix raw cocoa with ordinary cocoa or chocolate powder. Raw, organic cocoa powder consists of 100 percent cocoa and has not been exposed to excessively high temperatures, at which many nutrients disappear. Store the cocoa powder in a cool, dry place away from direct sunlight. An unopened bag will keep for up to two years.

GINGER. Contains a lot of antioxidants that boost the immune system, plus potassium, calcium, magnesium, phosphorus, copper, manganese, zinc, and vitamins C, E, and B6. When you buy fresh ginger you should look for a root that has firm flesh and has not begun to shrivel. Ginger has long been known as a cheap and effective remedy for travel sickness. It is also believed to regulate the blood sugar and have an anti-inflammatory effect on stiff joints and various types of joint pain. Ginger also boosts the body's consumption of heat and energy, which can aid weight loss. Fresh, unpeeled ginger can be stored in the refrigerator at 45–55 °F / 8–12 °C, preferably in a plastic bag or plastic box so that it does not dry out. It will keep for three months. Fresh ginger is also excellent for freezing, grated or whole. In that form it will keep for ever and it is very easy to grate straight from the freezer.

HERBS, FRESH. Sniff the herbs you buy and judge how they smell. When you use fresh herbs you can reckon that a tablespoon is approximately equivalent to a teaspoon of dried herbs. If you are buying herbs in a pot it is best to replant them and water them a lot as that way they will last longer. Bunches of herbs are best stored in a plastic bag in the refrigerator. Wash only those you are going to use, otherwise they will not keep well. Herbs last about a year in the freezer.

LICORICE. A sweet that does not need added sugar because it contains natural sweetness. According to health experts licorice should be eaten in moderation, otherwise it can cause salt balance disorders, high blood pressure, oedema, weight gain, and headaches.

SAFFRON. Sold as a powder, liquid concentrate, or whole strands. If you buy saffron strands you are guaranteed the genuine article. Crumble the strands between your fingers or grind them with a pestle and mortar before using. Saffron is toxic in large quantities and the recommended maximum daily dose is roughly equivalent to a large pinch (1.5 grams).

TURMERIC. Has anti-inflammatory and highly antioxidant properties that counteract inflammation and damage caused by so-called free radicals. Also said to be good for arteriosclerosis, Alzheimer's, diseases of the pancreas and liver, and certain forms of cancer. Turmeric is the name of both a species in the zingiberaceous plant family and of products made from the plant. It is the root that is boiled, dried, and ground into a yellowish powder. The taste is slightly bitter and somewhat reminiscent of ginger. Turmeric gives a strong yellow color to some kinds of curry and is sometimes used as a cheap way of making saffron go further. Store in a dry, dark place in a closed pack. Over time it can develop a musty taste so it is best to buy small quantities.

VANILLA. This is a popular flavoring that goes well with smoothies. Genuine vanilla powder is made from ground, dried vanilla pods. The pods are the fruit of the vanilla orchid, which is chiefly cultivated on Madagascar. Genuine vanilla powder can be used in the same way as vanilla sugar or vanilla extract. It is best to buy organic.

LIQUID BASES

There are many liquid bases to choose from when you want to make smoothies. Some are easy to make yourself, for example oat milk and various kinds of nut milk. When you buy readymade products, remember that they may contain high levels of added sugar.

ALMOND MILK. This contains 20 percent protein and masses of fiber, and is particularly rich in vitamin E, iron, zinc, calcium, magnesium, potassium, and phosphorus. Unsweetened almond milk can be bought readymade in shops but can also be made at home by blending almonds or almond butter with water. You will find recipes for homemade almond milk on page 40. Beware of readymade, sweetened almond milk that contains a lot of sugar. Almond milk freezes well in ice cube trays.

CHAMOMILE INFUSION. This is usually made from dried or fresh flowers, one to two teaspoons of dried herbs for a large cup, depending on how strong you want it. It is said to be good for both external and internal complaints and to be anti-inflammatory, disinfectant, and antispasmodic. The infusion is also sudorific and soothing. It is drunk as an evening tisane, as a remedy for fevers and colds, and for respiratory problems, cystitis, colic, and other gastric problems. It is also gargled for throat infections and applied to external abscesses, wounds, and other skin problems. The flowers can be used to make bathwater aromatic. In former times chamomile was placed in cradles to stop the devil exchanging babies. It should be kept in a dark dry place, not above normal room temperature. Chamomile infusion should be drunk in moderation because of the risk of allergy, and it should not be drunk at all by people who are allergic to plants of the daisy family.

COCONUT MILK. Rich in potassium, iron, magnesium, and phosphorus. The fat content may vary but is usually around 25 percent. Always buy unsweetened coconut milk with no additives. You can make small quantities of coconut milk yourself by blending grated coconut with water and then straining off the coconut flesh. Coconut milk freezes well in ice cube trays.

COCONUT WATER. This is the clear liquid that you find in a young, green coconut. Coconut water is 95 percent water, the rest is nutrients and minerals such as vitamin B, vitamin C, phosphorus, calcium, and zinc. Coconut water is extra rich in potassium and is sometimes called "nature's own sports drink." Coconut water is excellent for freezing in ice cube trays and will keep for six months in the freezer.

KOMBUCHA TEA. Contains lactic acid bacteria, acetic acid, polysaccharide, and vitamins C, E, K, B1, B2, B3, B6, and B12 among other things, plus the minerals iron, sodium, manganese, magnesium, potassium, copper, and zinc. The tea is made from the fermented kombucha mushroom (also called Volga mushroom or tea mushroom.) You can buy kombucha in health food shops, and there are various flavors. If you can obtain a kombucha culture you can also make and flavor your own tea. Kombucha tea freezes well in ice cube trays.

NUT MILK. Made of soaked and blended nuts, for example almonds, cashew nuts, hazelnuts, and walnuts. Nut milk is sold in well-stocked supermarkets and health food shops but you can also make it yourself. Beware of the ones with added sweeteners. Nut milk freezes well in ice cube trays.

OAT MILK. Made from oat flakes and water. It contains a lot of vitamin B1, iron, and antioxidants. Some manufacturers also add vitamin D obtained from sheep's wool, so vegans should be careful. A number of naturally occurring enzymes, vitamin A, and vitamin B12 are also often added. Oat milk is easy to make yourself, see page 40 for the recipe. An opened pack keeps for a couple of days in the refrigerator. This milk freezes well in ice cube trays.

RICE MILK. Made from brown rice. Rice milk has a low fat content and is lactose, cholesterol, and sugar free. It freezes well in ice cube trays.

ROOIBOS TEA. Contains among other things zinc, magnesium, calcium, manganese, and fluoride and is also a powerful antioxidant that is believed to counteract the unwanted effects of aging. Tea made from rooibos should draw for 6–8 minutes, in contrast to ordinary tea it does not develop the substances that make the drink bitter. Also it does not contain any stimulating theine (caffeine). Rooibos is sold in most supermarkets. It is best to choose an organic tea.

SOYMILK. Made from soybeans. This is the plant milk with the highest proportion of protein. Soymilk is also rich in vitamin E and lecithin. Apart from milk there are also soy ice cream and soy yoghurt, which is also good in smoothies. You can make your own soymilk from soy flour. The milk freezes well in ice cube trays.

NUTS AND SEEDS

ALMONDS. These are good after training since they are rich in energy and help to build muscle. Sweet almonds contain some healthy monounsaturated fat plus a lot of protein and vitamin E. In smoothies it can be a good idea to use almond butter, which can be bought in health food shops.

BRAZIL NUTS. In addition to a lot of protein, these contain selenium and zinc. The nuts consist of 70 percent fat. A large part of this fat is omega-6 and a small part omega-3. The nuts should be white inside. A yellowish color means that the fats have begun to turn rancid.

CHIA SEED. This seed is rich in omega-3, ALA (alpha-linolenic-acid), fiber, and protein. Two tablespoons contain more omega-3 than a whole salmon fillet. Chia seeds also contain a lot of healthy mineral substances, such as phosphorus, calcium, and potassium. Like linseed, chia seed is gelatinous, which means that it has a thick consistency when mixed with liquid. The recommended daily intake is two tablespoons. It is best to buy organic chia seed.

HAZELNUTS. Contain large quantities of vitamin E and protein as well as some fats.

HEMP SEED. Contains high levels of both healthy polyunsaturated fatty acids, omega-3, and omega-6. The seeds consist of at least 25 percent protein and are rich in vital amino acids. They also contain high levels of calcium, magnesium, phosphorus, sulfur, carotene, iron, zinc, and vitamins C, E, B1, B2, B3, and B6. Hemp seed is available in various different forms shelled, unshelled, or as hemp protein powder, which works extremely well as a natural protein supplement.

LINSEED. Contains among other things vitamin B, and minerals such as iron, phosphorus, potassium, calcium, zinc, and magnesium. In the stomach it forms a layer of jelly that facilitates digestion. Linseed is available whole or crushed. You should limit your intake of crushed linseed particularly. Some experts recommend a maximum of two tablespoons a day.

PECAN NUTS. These are drupes that grow on a tree of the hickory family. The nuts contain 72 percent fat, of which 63 percent is unsaturated. They also contain large quantities of antioxidants. Much of the nutritional value is found in the brown inner skin.

PINE NUTS. Contain a lot of zinc, iron, protein, and polyunsaturated fat.

PISTACHIO NUTS. Contain a lot of fat and protein. These are not nuts but seeds, and therefore they can often be eaten by people with a nut allergy. Sometimes the shell is colored red to hide blemishes. Avoid these and try to buy uncolored nuts instead.

PSYLLIUM SEEDS. These are very rich in fiber and have good absorption capacity. When the fiber comes into contact with liquid a jelly-like substance is formed that causes the seeds to swell to more than ten times their original volume. In that way they quickly fill the stomach and give a feeling of fullness without supplying too many calories. The jelly also has a softening and lubricating function, which facilitates passage through the intestine and prevents constipation. Research suggests that a diet including psyllium seeds can stabilize the blood sugar and reduce cholesterol. Psyllium seeds should always be taken with plenty of water to prevent their getting stuck in the throat. The recommended daily dose is one to two tablespoons.

PUMPKIN SEEDS. Contain zinc and antioxidants, among other things. They have a high protein content and contain a lot of polyunsaturated fat. Pumpkin seeds are also anti-inflammatory and boost the immune system.

SESAME SEEDS. Contain 50 percent fat, almost all of which is healthy. The seeds also have a high protein content of 18 percent. Sesame seed paste is good in smoothies and is sold in health food shops.

SUNFLOWER SEEDS. These come from the center of the sunflower and are rich in vitamin E, omega-6, and monounsaturated fatty acids. They also contain vitamin B5, which is thought to help the body handle stress.

WALNUTS. These are very nutritious, especially for vegetarians, as they contain large quantities of omega-3.

MAKE YOUR OWN NUT MILK

For preference choose unsalted, unroasted, and organic nuts and seeds. They taste best and contain the most nutrients. Soak the nuts and leave them to stand in a cool place overnight to remove indigestible enzymes and give the milk a milder taste. Strain off the water and rinse the nuts thoroughly. Blend with fresh water until the nuts are really finely ground. Hazelnuts do not need to be soaked since they do not contain enzyme inhibitors. Coconut flakes and shelled hemp seeds can also be blended without soaking.

Strain the milk in a nut milk bag or fine sieve (shelled hemp seeds do not need to be strained). Squeeze out as much liquid as possible. Keep the milk in a glass container because it will keep longer there than in a plastic bottle, about three to five days in the refrigerator. Nut milk freezes extremely well in ice cube trays. You can flavor nut milk with vanilla, cinnamon, or cardamom, or sweeten it with medjool dates or agave syrup. The nut mass that is left can be saved for making nut balls, muesli, and bread, or for mixing in porridge.

ALMOND MILK
1 cup / 150 g soaked almonds + 4 cups/ 1 liter water + pinch of salt

CASHEW MILK
1 cup/ 130 g soaked cashew nuts + 4 cups/ 1 liter water + pinch of salt

COCONUT MILK
1 cup / 90 g shredded coconut + 4 cups/ 1 liter water + pinch of salt

HAZELNUT MILK
1 cup / 140 g hazelnuts + 4 cups/ 1 liter water + pinch of salt

HEMP MILK
4 tsp shelled hemp seeds + 4 cups/ 1 liter water + pinch of salt

OAT MILK
1 cup / 90 g soaked rolled oats + 4 cups/ 1 liter water + pinch of salt

SESAME MILK
1 cup / 130 g soaked sesame seeds + 4 cups/ 1 liter water + 1 pinch of salt

SOYMILK
generous ¾ cup / 175 g soaked soybeans or 4 tsp / 20 ml soy flour + 4¼ cups/ 1 liter water + pinch of salt

CARROT, ORANGE, & CAYENNE PEPPER

Chili can seem addictive. That is because the substance that makes the chili strong, capsaicin, boosts the production of endorphins in the body. Endorphins have an analgesic effect and induce feelings of wellbeing and relaxation—it's not surprising that we sometimes feel a strong desire for chili.

Cayenne pepper is a type of chili that has been found to have several good properties: it increases the metabolic rate, dissolves mucus, and is generally good for the digestion; it cleanses the body of toxins, is bactericidal, lowers the blood pressure, is effective against cardiovascular disease and cancer, and thins the blood. It is good for angina sufferers (just like garlic it dilates the blood vessels, amongst other things). Cayenne pepper can even be sprinkled on wounds to stem bleeding.

2 glasses of smoothie

2 tbsp goji berries

1¼ cups / 300 ml freshly pressed carrots

3 oranges

½ lime

1 banana, frozen (see page 12)

1 pinch cayenne pepper

sweetener to taste

generous ¾ cup / 100 ml ice (optional)

Soak the goji berries in carrot juice for 5–10 minutes. Press the oranges and the lime. Blend all the ingredients to a smooth consistency and season with cayenne pepper. Blend in the ice for a chilled smoothie.

STRAWBERRY & CHAMOMILE

Chamomile is one of the world's most widely used medicinal plants. It grows wild in fields and on verges in many countries and is chiefly picked for the medicinal properties of the daisy-like flowers. Chamomile contains several active medicinal substances and essential oils—among other things the blue colorant chamazulene. Chamomile can be used both externally and internally for anti-inflammatory, bactericidal, and sudorific purposes. In addition the flower has tranquilizing and sedative properties.

The dried or fresh flowers are usually used for infusions: one to two teaspoons of the dried herb for a large cup depending on the strength required. It is good for irritation of the stomach or intestines, gastritis, and colicky pains. For menstrual pain women can drink a couple of cups to alleviate cramp. Chamomile tisane can also alleviate tension headaches and mild migraine, and is believed to have both preventive and healing effects on colds. If you find it hard to relax in the evening a cup of chamomile tisane can help calm you.

If you are allergic to plants of the daisy family you should not use chamomile.

Take 2 tsp chamomile for 1¼ cups / 300 ml chamomile tisane.

---

2 glasses of smoothie

3 cups / 300 g strawberries, frozen
½ cup / 50 g dried mulberries
1¼ cups / 300 ml chamomile tisane, cooled
juice of half a lemon
sweetener to taste
2 tsp chia seeds

Blend the strawberries, mulberries, tisane, and freshly squeezed lemon juice to a smooth consistency. Taste it and sweeten if needed. Add the chia seeds and blend for a few more seconds until the seeds are evenly distributed.

BUCKTHORN, MANGO, & STRAWBERRY

Buckthorn grows wild but in recent years commercial planting has become more and more common in the USA and Canada, and in Scandinavia, Eastern Europe, and Asia. The plant is dioecious, which means there are male and female versions. The female plant produces berries but only after it has been pollinated by a male plant. The male plants may also produce berries but usually only in small quantities. Since pollination is carried out by the wind a good mixture of male and female plants is essential for a supply of berries.

---

2 glasses of smoothie

1 cup / 100 g buckthorn berries (frozen or fresh)

1 cup / 200 g mango (frozen or fresh)

2 cups / 200 g strawberries (frozen or fresh)

1 banana

generous ¾ cup / 200 ml freshly pressed apple juice

generous ¾ cup / 200 ml water

generous ¾ cup—1⅔ cups / 100–200 ml ice (if you are using fresh fruit)

Blend all the ingredients apart from the ice to a smooth consistency. Blend in ice for a chilled smoothie. Serve in tall glasses with straws and decorate with a few buckthorn berries.

ROSE HIP, PINEAPPLE, & PAPAYA

In popular medicine rose hips are used to treat scurvy, in other words vitamin C deficiency. Rose hips have also been used to treat constipation, tiredness, joint problems, diverticulitis, emphysema, ear problems, hemorrhoids, bladder problems, colic, stiffness, and problems of the back, legs, feet, and neck. Rose hips are not only used to treat people, they are also given to horses to boost their immune systems.

Whole rose hip powder is made from whole dried rose hips and contains sixty times more vitamin C than citrus fruit. In addition it is rich in antioxidants and vital minerals, such as iron, calcium, potassium, and magnesium. Rose hips also contain a lot of folic acid, which is particularly good for women who are breastfeeding, pregnant, or trying to conceive. Rose hip powder is easy to make yourself: dry whole rose hips and grind them to a powder.

---

2 glasses of smoothie

3 tsp rose hip powder (dried, ground rose hips)

1 cup / 200 g pineapple, chopped (frozen or fresh)

½ cup / 100 g papaya, chopped

juice of half a lemon

generous ⅔ cup / 200 ml freshly pressed apple juice

7 tbsp / 100 ml water

generous ¾ cup—1⅔ cups / 100–200 ml crushed ice (if you are using fresh fruit)

Blend all the ingredients apart from the ice to a smooth consistency. Blend in the ice for a chilled smoothie. Serve in large glasses with straws. Sprinkle with a little rose hip powder or decorate with fresh rose hips if they are in season.

WATERMELON, RASPBERRY, & MINT

Watermelon is one of the few foods that contain considerable quantities of the powerful antioxidant lycopene, which is said to reduce the risk of heart disease and certain types of cancer—for example cervical and prostate cancer. Watermelon is also a good source of vitamin A, vitamin C, and vitamin B6.

There are many kinds of watermelon. Most of them have dark pink to red flesh but there are also some varieties that have a yellowish color. The watermelon is round to oval in shape and weighs between 2 and 20 lb / 2 and 20 kg. Most varieties taste roughly similar but there can be considerable differences in sweetness. I prefer the big, oval watermelons with red flesh.

Choose melons with no cracks or blemishes. The skin should be firm, smooth, and yellow on the underside where the melon has ripened against the soil. Ripe watermelons have a slight aroma and should feel quite heavy—they are 92 percent water.

---

2 glasses of smoothie

3⅓ cups / 500 g watermelon, cubed (approx. ¼ medium-size watermelon

1 cup / 120 g raspberries (frozen or fresh)

juice of half a lime

5–6 mint leaves

generous ¾ cup—1⅔ cups / 100–200 ml crushed ice

sweetener to taste

Split the watermelon, remove the pits and scoop out the flesh. Add the raspberries, lime juice, and mint leaves. Blend until you have a smooth consistency. Then blend in the ice for a chilled smoothie. Serve in large glasses and decorate with raspberries.

MANGO, ORANGE, & ROSE HIP

The mango is India's and Pakistan's national fruit and it is rich in several groups of antioxidants, such as beta-carotene, vitamin C, and also potassium. Mango is especially rich in beta-carotene, which is converted to vitamin A in the body. Vitamin A is good for the eyesight, skeleton, skin, mucous membranes, and immune system. Apart from its beneficial effects on the body, beta-carotene is also very good for the skin. The antioxidant vitamin C also fortifies the blood vessels, skin, teeth, and skeleton. Like cashew nuts, mangos contain the substance urushiol and people with allergies should be a little careful, at least when handling the skin.

When it is in season you can freeze mango in portions in plastic bags. It is much cheaper and tastier to eat the frozen fruit when it is not in season than to eat fruit that has been picked unripe, stored for a long time, and sprayed with various agents to keep it fresh for months. Fresh newly picked fruit is always best but freshly picked fruit that has been frozen immediately also works well. To select a good mango, smell it and squeeze it carefully to see if it yields.

---

2 glasses of smoothie

4 oranges

½ lime

1½ cups / 300 g frozen mango (or 1 fresh mango)

2 tbsp whole rose hip powder (dried, ground rose hips)

generous ¾ cup—1⅔ cups / 100–200 ml crushed ice (if you are using fresh fruit)

Press the oranges and the lime. Make sure that no pits get through as they can give a bitter taste. Peel the mango with a potato peeler and cut it into pieces, don't forget it has a big pit. Blend the newly pressed juice, mango, and rose hip powder to a smooth consistency. Blend in the ice for a chilled smoothie. Serve in large glasses and decorate with a little diced mango or rose hip powder.

KIWIFRUIT & MANGO

Rinse the kiwifruit. The skin is fine to eat. It is soft and tasty and you do not feel the hairs in your mouth. Also the skin is nutritious. The kiwifruit contains large quantities of vitamin C and also vitamin E. The kiwifruit does not mix well with dairy products and should be mixed with berry fruit and tropical fruit.

The kiwi was called the Chinese gooseberry until the 1960s. Kiwifruit are commonly imported from New Zealand but we can also obtain them from Mediterranean countries, during the period from November to April. A good kiwifruit should yield to light pressure if you squeeze it. Beware of overripe kiwifruit, which may have a nasty taste.

---

2 glasses of smoothie

2 oranges

juice of half a lime

3 kiwifruit

1½ cups / 300 g frozen mango
(or 1 fresh mango), chopped

generous ¾ cup / 200 ml ice cold water

Press the oranges and the lime. Peel and chop the kiwifruit. Blend all the ingredients to a smooth consistency. Do not blend too long as the black kiwifruit seeds give a very bitter taste if they are crushed in the blender and left to stand for a little while.

PINEAPPLE & STRAWBERRY

This sweet and tasty smoothie contains a lot of nutritious dietary fiber and vitamins that protect against viruses and infections. Above all, pineapple is rich in vitamin C, which builds up the connective tissues and helps the body to absorb iron from food. Vitamin C is also an antioxidant that protects against free radicals, which have a damaging effect on the body's cells. Apart from the vitamins, pineapple is rich in the enzyme bromelain, which is very powerful when it comes to breaking down proteins—which in turn facilitates digestion. Bromelain is also good for the circulation and lowers blood pressure.

To find a good pineapple you should look for a plump one. To see whether it is ripe, you can test by carefully pulling off a leaf that is quite far down. If it comes off the pineapple is ripe, but it may be overripe, so you can try to choose a pineapple whose leaf does not come off and leave it to ripen at home.

2 glasses of smoothie

½ pineapple, chopped
 (approx. 2 cups / 400 g frozen)

2 cups / 200 g strawberries
 (fresh or frozen)

juice of half a lime

generous ¾ cup /200 ml ice cold water

generous ¾ cup—1⅓ cups / 100–
 200 ml crushed ice (optional)

Split the pineapple and cut out the hard middle part. Pinch the stalks off the strawberries if they are fresh ones. Press the lime. Make sure that you do not get any pits because they can produce a bitter taste. Blend the ingredients to a smooth, thick consistency. Blend in the ice if you are using fresh strawberries to make a chilled smoothie.

TIP! Juice made from pineapple and strawberries is also delicious, but in that case do not add water and process all the ingredients in a juicer instead.

REDCURRANTS & MANGO

Redcurrants contain plenty of vitamins C and K, potassium, and masses of fiber. Currants are normally grown in gardens but a wild subspecies of currant grows in some northern areas—you just go out in the forest and pick them! You can make a nice wine from both the wild and the cultivated fruit. Currants are usually in season in August and they freeze extremely well.

---

2 glasses of smoothie

generous 2 cups / 200 g redcurrants (fresh or frozen)

generous 2 cups / 200 g strawberries (fresh or frozen)

1 mango (or 1½ cups / 300 g frozen mango)

generous ¾ cup / 200 ml freshly pressed apple juice

generous ¾ cup—1⅔ cups / 100–200 ml crushed ice (if you are using fresh fruit)

Rinse the currants, take the stalks off the strawberries, and remove any stalks from the currants. Peel the mango with a potato peeler and cut it into pieces—don't forget it has a big pit. Blend everything apart from the ice to a smooth consistency. Blend in the ice for a chilled smoothie. Serve in large glasses and decorate with a sprig of redcurrants.

STRAWBERRY & CHILI

Chili gets the metabolism going. Different chilis have different strengths so you need to be a bit careful. Common varieties include the Spanish pepper, birdseye pepper, habanero pepper, perennial Spanish pepper, and rocoto pepper. Dried chili is sold in tins or packs and works almost as well as fresh. But watch the strength!

The hotness in the chili is not in the seeds but in the mesophyll walls and the pericarp. To reduce the strength you can split the chili lengthways and scrape out the inside with a knife. The substance that makes chilis strong is called capsaicin and is a non-water soluble oil. If it is too hot in your mouth drinking some water will not help. On the other hand capsaicin is fat soluble, so nuts (for example) give relief.

---

2 glasses of smoothie

4 cups / 400 g strawberries (fresh or frozen)

chili to taste (start with a small piece)

juice of 1 lime

generous ¾ cup / 200 ml freshly pressed apple juice

generous ¾ cup—1⅓ cups / 100–200 ml crushed ice (if you are using fresh fruit)

sweetener to taste

Pinch the stalks off the strawberries. Split the chili lengthways, remove the seeds and the white membranes, and chop. Blend all the ingredients to a smooth consistency. Blend in ice for a chilled smoothie. Add a little sweetener if you think it needs it.

TIP! Swap the strawberries for mango, that is also super delicious! Strawberries and mangos go extremely well with chili.

ORANGE & BANANA

Most people know that oranges contain a lot of vitamin C, but it is perhaps not equally well known that they also contain a number of other useful substances that an effervescent tablet cannot give you. Apart from boosting the immune system, lowering the blood pressure, and protecting against colds and infections, oranges provide extra protection against eye disease, rheumatism, cardiovascular disease, and cancer. In addition the vitamin C in oranges is revitalizing for the skin.

Vitamin C makes it easier for the body to absorb several nutrients, for instance iron, zinc, copper, calcium, and vitamin B9 (folic acid). Vitamin C also has an antioxidant effect on other substances in the body and helps to break down harmful free radicals. Vitamin C cannot be stored in the body but needs to be supplied every day.

---

2 glasses of smoothie

4 oranges

½ lemon

2 bananas

generous ¾ cup—1⅔ cups / 100–200 ml crushed ice (optional)

Press the oranges and half lemon. Make sure that no pits get in as they can produce a bitter taste. Blend with the bananas to a smooth, thick consistency. Blend in the ice for a chilled smoothie.

TIP! Add a few strawberries or raspberries for a beautiful color and an unusual flavor.

POMEGRANATE & GRAPEFRUIT

Pomegranates are a super fruit that originated in Persia and has been cultivated for thousands of years. Pomegranates are rich above all in folic acid and antioxidants, such as vitamin C, carotene, gallocatechins, and anthocyanin (which gives the pomegranate its pink color). The antioxidants build up the body's cells and help to prevent disease. Folic acid is important for the growth of new cells and is required for the formation of red blood corpuscles.

Do you find it hard to get the nutritious pomegranate seeds out? This is how you do it: roll the pomegranate against a hard surface, cut it in half, and hold the halves upside down over a basin, at the same time banging the skin with a wooden spoon—hey presto! Pomegranates can be bought fresh during the winter but you can use frozen or dried pomegranate seeds when they are not in season.

---

2 glasses of smoothie

2 pomegranates (or 1¼ cups /
200 g frozen, or 3 tbsp dried seeds)

2 pink grapefruit

2 oranges

1⅔ cups / 200 ml crushed ice

Divide the pomegranates and press them in a citrus press—you can blend the pomegranate seeds instead if they are frozen or if you want extra fiber. Cut the segments out of the grapefruit and throw away the bitter membranes and the peel. Press the oranges and blend with the rest of the ingredients. Serve with a few pomegranate seeds as decoration.

TIP! If you do not have the time or energy to cut out the grapefruit segments, it works just as well if you press the grapefruit in a citrus press.

RASPBERRY & PEAR

Pears contain twice as much fiber as apples. On the other hand pears have a shorter shelf-life, so it is a good idea to buy unripe pears and keep them in the refrigerator for a few days before they are to be used. If you want to speed up the process you can place the pears in a paper bag with an apple—apples give off ethylene gas, which makes other fruit ripen more quickly.

Fiber is an essential ingredient in our diet. It helps to keep the blood sugar level down and facilitates digestion. A diet with a lot of fiber reduces the risk of cancer and also counteracts cholesterol. Apart from fiber, pears are rich in potassium, riboflavin, and vitamins A and C.

---

2 glasses of smoothie

3 ripe pears

scant 2 cups / 200 g raspberries, frozen

7 tbsp / 100 ml freshly pressed apple juice

generous ¾ cup / 200 ml ice cold water

sweetener to taste

Cut the pears into quarters and cut out the cores. Blend the pieces of pear with the raspberries, juice, and water until the consistency is even and smooth—the harder the pears, the longer they take to blend. Taste and sweeten as required. Serve with raspberries.

TROPICAL FRUIT

Papaya is rich in vitamins A, C, E, and B and antioxidants such as carotene, zeaxanthin, and flavonoids. There are also several important minerals in papaya, such as potassium, magnesium, calcium, and iron. Papaya contains the enzyme papain, which is used in medicine for digestive problems. Papaya is also said to be useful for losing weight.

2 glasses of smoothie

2 tbsp dried goji berries

1¼ cups / 300 ml coconut water

½ cup / 100 g papaya, frozen

½ cup / 100 g pineapple, frozen

½ cup / 100 g mango, frozen

1 banana

Leave the goji berries to soften in the coconut water for 5–10 minutes. Blend all the ingredients to a chilled smoothie. Decorate with a few goji berries.

TIP! It works very well if you replace the frozen fruit with a tropical fruit mix, which you may find on the frozen counter.

CARROT, PINEAPPLE, & GOJI BERRIES

Carrots contain beta-carotene, which is a precursor to vitamin A. Vitamin A and carotene prevent cataracts and age-related macular degeneration, and are said to be helpful for seeing in the dark. A deficiency in vitamin A can cause night blindness. Carrots are also good for the skin.

Carrots are best stored without their leaves, in a plastic bag in the refrigerator or a cool room. The leaves should be cut off since otherwise they will steal nutrition and cause the carrot to go soft.

---

2 glasses of smoothie

3 tbsp goji berries

1¼ cups / 300 ml freshly pressed carrot juice

1 cup / 200 g pineapple, frozen

juice of half a lime

Leave the goji berries to soften in the carrot juice for 5–10 minutes. Blend to a smooth consistency. Serve with a slice of pineapple or carrot as a garnish.

PINEAPPLE, GOJI BERRIES, & REDCURRANTS

In order to be allowed to call juice juice, it must consist of 100 percent pure fruit juice. Home-pressed juice is the freshest you can get and it keeps for only up to one day. Juice that is described as freshly pressed is made from fresh fruit and vegetables—it keeps for only a short time after it has been pressed. Freshly pressed not from concentrate juice is juice that has been pressed from freshly picked fruit in its country of origin and is pressed on the spot. In order to make sure it doesn't go bad during transportation, it is pasteurized a number of times. Certain kinds are deep frozen to extend their shelf-life. Some are called juice from concentrate, which means that the water is taken out of the juice so that only the concentrate remains, the concentrate then becomes aseptic and keeps for a year, and in factories water and natural flavorings are added to produce a drinkable juice. Fruit drinks and nectars are not juice, but a mixture of water, sugar, sometimes artificial sweeteners, concentrate, and other additives—beware of these! I usually choose to press the juice myself, and when the fruit is in season I press and freeze it either in ice cube trays or freezer containers, depending on the quantity and what I intend to use it for. I quite often buy freshly pressed juice when I don't have time, but I very very rarely have concentrate in my shopping trolley.

---

2 glasses of smoothie

2 tbsp dried goji berries

1 tbsp shelled hemp seeds

⅔ cup / 150 ml freshly pressed pineapple juice

⅔ cup / 150 ml coconut water

⅔ cup / 150 g pineapple, frozen

1½ cups / 150 g redcurrants (frozen or fresh)

Soak the goji berries and hemp seeds in the pineapple juice for 5–10 minutes. Blend all the ingredients to a chilled smoothie.

NECTARINE, RASPBERRY, & MULBERRY

Mulberry contains a lot of vitamin C, vitamin K, iron, and calcium. Mulberries are also a good source of resveratrol, an antioxidant and anticoagulant that has a number of beneficial effects on health. Mulberries are considered to boost the kidneys and liver and to be good for the hair and eyes. Studies have shown that the berries can stabilize the blood sugar level and increase the level of good cholesterol. The recommended daily dose is 3 tbsp / 20–30 g. You can find dried mulberries in most well-stocked supermarkets and health food shops. It is best to buy organic.

---

2 glasses of smoothie

3 ripe nectarines

scant 1 cup / 100 g raspberries, frozen

½ cup / 50 g mulberries, dried

2 tbsp chia seeds

generous ¾ cup / 200 ml almond milk

sweetener to taste

Remove the pits from the nectarines and blend all the ingredients to a smooth consistency. Taste and sweeten if necessary. Decorate with raspberries or mulberries.

STRAWBERRY, KOMBUCHA, & MULBERRY

Kombucha tea is a Chinese health drink with an extremely long history. The tea was drunk as long ago as 200 BCE, and according to its advocates it has many health-giving properties, among others improved digestion, softer skin, and reduced pain in the body and joints. Kombucha also alleviates hunger pangs and problems with the stomach and intestines—for example wind, constipation, and side effects from medical treatment. The drink is said to boost the immune system, which helps protect against colds and influenza. Among other things kombucha tea contains lactic acid bacteria, acetic acid, polysaccharide, and vitamins C, E, K, B1, B2, B3, B6, and B12, plus the minerals iron, sodium, manganese, magnesium, potassium, copper, and zinc.

Kombucha tea is produced from the fermented kombucha mushroom (also called the Volga mushroom or tea mushroom). The mushroom varies in color from pale and transparent to brown. The drink is made by mixing yeast and bacteria cultures with sugar and tea (black, green, or oolong), which is then left to ferment for about 10 days. Readymade kombucha is sold in health food shops and is available in various flavors. If you can obtain kombucha culture you can make your own tea and flavor it as you wish.

According to traditional Chinese medicine, kombucha tea is believed to be the drink of immortality and the elixir of life.

---

2 glasses of smoothie

2 tbsp dried goji berries

3 tbsp dried mulberries

1 tbsp chia seeds

1⅔ cups / 400 ml kombucha tea (bought or homemade)

2 cups / 200 g strawberries, frozen

Soak the goji berries, mulberries, and chia seeds in the kombucha tea for 5–10 minutes. Blend to an even paste. Add the strawberries and blend to a chilled smoothie. Serve with strawberries, goji berries, or mulberries on top.

LINGON BERRY, ORANGE, & GOJI BERRY

Lingon berries have a high content of vitamins A, B, and C, plus the minerals potassium, calcium, phosphorus, and iron. Lingon berries are bactericidal and, just like cranberries, they are therefore thought to be useful against urinary infections. The berries also neutralize the smell of urine. Lingon berries may help those with gastric ulcers and gingivitis. Lingon used to be sold in the drugstore, amongst other things as an antipyretic.

---

2 glasses of smoothie

2 oranges

3 tbsp goji berries, dried

2 ripe pears

1½ cups / 200 g lingon berries
   (fresh or frozen)

2 tbsp linseed oil

¾–1⅔ cups / 100–200 ml crushed ice
   (if you are using fresh fruit)

sweetener to taste

Squeeze the oranges. Soak the goji berries in orange juice for 5–10 minutes. Cut the pears in quarters and remove the cores. Blend all the ingredients except the ice to a smooth consistency. Blend in the ice for a chilled smoothie. Taste and sweeten if necessary. Decorate with a few lingon berries on the top.

TIP! If you cannot find fresh or frozen lingon berries, freeze-dried berry powder is available from health food shops. The lingon berries can also be replaced with cranberries.

BLUEBERRY, RASPBERRY, & GOJI BERRY

Blueberries are powerful antioxidants and are sometimes called super berries. They are good for the skin and night vision, and for those with cataracts. Blueberries are also said to be good for the circulation in the legs and to protect against varicose veins, inflammations, blood clots, high blood pressure, and bad LDL cholesterol. The berries are considered good for diabetics since they are thought to help to regulate the blood sugar. Blueberries are also good for urinary infections and diarrhea.

Wild blueberries are extra nutritious and contain plenty of flavonoids, carotene, vitamin C, vitamin B6, and magnesium.

---

2 glasses of smoothie

3 tbsp goji berries, dried

2 tbsp chia seeds

5–6 dates, pits removed

generous ¾ cup / 200 ml green tea, cooled

1½ cups / 150 g blueberries, frozen

1½ cups / 150 g raspberries, frozen

Soak the goji berries, chia seeds, and dates in green tea for 5–10 minutes. Blend to a smooth purée. Add the berries and blend to make a chilled smoothie. Decorate with raspberries and blueberries.

BLUEBERRY, BLACKBERRY, & BEETS

Beets contain calcium, vitamin C, iron, magnesium, phosphorus, and manganese amongst other things. Beets cleanse the blood and stimulate the growth of red blood cells. Studies have shown that beets increase the body's ability to absorb oxygen and its stamina in physical exercise. Beets are also thought to help against high blood pressure and gastric ulcers and in cleansing the gut, liver, and gall bladder of toxins.

---

2 glasses of smoothie

1¼ cups / 300 ml fresh pressed apple juice

1 small beet, raw

2 cups / 200 g blueberries, frozen

1 cup / 120 g blackberries, frozen

1 tbsp linseed

sweetener to taste

Rinse, peel, and chop the beet into small pieces. Blend with the apple juice until the consistency is even and smooth. Add the rest of the ingredients and blend to a chilled smoothie. Taste and sweeten if required.

PINEAPPLE, PAPAYA, & LUCUMA

Lucuma is a nutritious fruit that tastes a little like toffee. The delicate fruit comes from a subtropical tree that grows high up in the Andes in South America. The soft sweetness of lucuma makes it an excellent alternative to ordinary sugar. Lucuma powder works perfectly in giving the smoothie an extra boost in both flavor and nutrients.

Lucuma does not just taste good. It is also rich in fiber, antioxidants, vitamins, and minerals—particularly vitamins C and B, beta-carotene, calcium, phosphorus, and iron. All the nutrients are preserved in lucuma powder, but in a concentrated form. The powder is available in well-stocked health food shops.

2 glasses of smoothie

3 tbsp dried goji berries

juice of 1 lime

generous ⅓ cup / 100 ml coconut water

1 cup / 200 g ripe papaya

1 cup / 200 g pineapple, frozen

½ banana

2 tbsp lucuma powder

generous ⅓ cup / 100 ml coconut milk

Soak the goji berries in the lime juice and coconut water for 5–10 minutes. Peel and de-seed the papaya. Blend all the ingredients to make a delicious and naturally sweet smoothie.

LINGON BERRY, MANGO, & ACAI BERRY

Acai is a super berry from South America's rainforests. It is stuffed with antioxidants, vitamins, and essential fats and contains high levels of vitamins B and C, minerals, fiber, and protein. The levels of potassium, calcium, iron, magnesium, copper, phosphorus, and zinc are unusually high compared with other fruit. Acai is rich in the useful antioxidant anthocyanin that also gives the berries their purple color.

The acai berry is really a drupe. Just 10 percent of the berry is edible, the rest is the pit. The flavor is rich and dark—a blend of blueberry, olive, and chocolate. As well as its rich content of vitamins and antioxidants (seven times as much as in the blueberry), the acai also contains good fatty acids.

Acai berries have become popular for adding to smoothies and juices, but since they quickly go stale they are usually sold as pasteurized juice. Unfortunately much of the nutritional value disappears in the pasteurization. Freeze-dried acai berry powder is therefore a better alternative if you cannot obtain fresh ones. The powder is available in well-stocked health food shops.

---

2 glasses of smoothie

½ cup / 100 g lingon berries (fresh or frozen)

¾ cup / 150 g mango, frozen

2 tbsp acai berry powder

generous ¾ cup / 200 ml coconut water

generous ⅓ cup / 100 ml freshly pressed apple juice

Blend all the ingredients to make a chilled smoothie.

APRICOT, RASPBERRY, & CHAMOMILE

Apricot is known as *Prunus armeniaca* in Latin—in other words Armenian plum. These days we know that the fruit itself comes from China, where it was already being cultivated 4,000–5,000 years ago. Today 85 percent of all apricots come from Turkey. Apricots are rich in dietary fiber, potassium, calcium, magnesium, and vitamin B6 amongst other things.

Since it is difficult to obtain fresh apricots for a large part of the year—finding ripe specimens seems to be almost impossible—you can instead use dried apricots. Just soak them for a while before using them.

2 glasses of smoothie

10 apricots (dried or fresh)

2 tbsp goji berries

1 tbsp chia seeds

1¼ cups / 300 ml chamomile infusion, cooled

scant 2 cups / 200 g raspberries, frozen

1 tbsp lucuma powder (optional)

Put the apricots, goji berries, and chia seeds to soak in the chamomile infusion for 5–10 minutes. Blend to an even purée. Add the raspberries and the lucuma powder, and blend to make a chilled smoothie.

GRAPE, STRAWBERRY, & LUCUMA

A grapefruit contains more vitamin C than the daily amount required for an adult. Pink or ruby grapefruit are sweeter in taste than the yellow ones. Grapefruit really boosts the immune system, gives you a lovely skin, and contains many restorative antioxidants that protect against both cardiovascular disease and cancer. Grapefruit is good for influenza, irritations of the mouth and throat, and for ear inflammation and urinary infections. It helps to lower the bad LDL cholesterol and may help to keep the blood pressure down. Crushed grapefruit seeds have fungicidal and bactericidal effects and can be used for fungal infections.

Grapefruit can affect the action of some medicines, particularly heart medicines and antihypertensives, so consult your doctor before eating grapefruit in conjunction with medicine.

---

2 glasses of smoothie

3 grapefruit

2 cups / 200 g strawberries, frozen

generous ¾ cup / 200 ml water

2 tbsp lucuma powder

2 tbsp dried mulberries

Separate the grapefruit into segments and throw away the bitter membranes and the peel. Add the other ingredients and blend to a smooth consistency.

TIP! If you do not have the time or the energy to separate the grapefruit segments, this works fine if you press the grapefruit in a citrus press.

RASPBERRY & MANGO

Raspberry contains large quantities of nutrients that keep us healthy and fit. These super berries are anti-inflammatory, boost the immune system, and are said to protect against cancer and heart disease. Raspberries are rich in fiber, which helps to keep the cholesterol levels down. This fruit contains a lot of vitamin C, folic acid, iron, calcium, and potassium. Raspberries are also mucolytic and detoxifying, and may alleviate menstrual pains.

Buy raspberries of an even color. They spoil easily and should be used within two days. Stock up during the season and freeze them. Health food shops often stock freeze-dried raspberry powder that works well when used in smoothies.

---

2 glasses of smoothie

1 small mango (or 1 cup / 200 g frozen)

juice of half a lime

1½ cups / 150 g raspberries (fresh or frozen)

generous ¾ cup / 200 ml coconut water

1 tbsp lucuma powder

1 tbsp hemp seed

Peel the mango with a potato peeler and cut it into pieces; remember that it has a big pit. Press the lime, and make sure that none of the seeds is included because they can give a bitter flavor. Blend all the ingredients to a smooth consistency.

TIP! You might like to try adding a little chili powder or chopped chili.

BLUEBERRY, COCONUT, & ACAI BERRY

Blueberry and coconut might seem a strange combination of flavors, but in a smoothie it is surprisingly tasty! For an added boost to the smoothie this recipe includes hemp seed for a mild, nutty flavor, and acai berry powder to provide an extra vitamin kick.

---

2 glasses of smoothie

1 banana

2 cups / 200 g blueberries, frozen

4 dates, pits removed

2 tbsp hemp seed, shelled

2 tbsp acai berry powder

2 tbsp coconut oil

1¼ cups / 300 ml coconut water

Blend all the ingredients to a creamy consistency. Serve with big straws and a few blueberries on top. Yum!

ALMOND CHOCOLATE WITH BANANA & VANILLA

Almonds are usually called nuts but in the botanical sense they are drupes and related to plums, peaches, and apricots amongst other things. The almond itself grows as a seed in the core of the fruit. Almonds contain 20 percent protein and masses of fiber, and are especially rich in vitamin E, iron, zinc, calcium, magnesium, potassium, and phosphorus, which make them perfect for smoothies to enjoy after a hard session at the gym.

You can buy unsweetened almond milk in shops, and you can also make your own by blending almonds or almond butter with water. If you make it yourself the milk has a higher almond content than the bought milk does. You will find the recipe for homemade almond milk on page 40. Beware of readymade sweetened almond milk that contains a lot of sugar!

---

2 glasses of smoothie

1⅔ cups / 400 ml almond milk (or 3 tbsp almond butter + 1½ cups / 350 ml water)

2 bananas

4–5 dates, pits removed

2 tbsp cocoa powder

2 tsp linseed oil (optional)

1 tsp vanilla extract

sweetener to taste

¾ –1⅔ cups / 100–200 ml crushed ice (if required)

almond flour for decorating

Blend all the ingredients except the ice to a smooth consistency. Blend in ice for a chilled smoothie. Serve in attractive glasses and sprinkle with almond flour.

CHOCOLATE, DATE, & TURMERIC

Turmeric has anti-inflammatory and highly antioxidant properties that counteract inflammation and damage caused by so-called free radicals—residual products formed in the oxygenation of the body.

Results from laboratory experiments have shown that turmeric protects against arteriosclerosis, Alzheimer's, and diseases of the pancreas, liver, and lungs. Turmeric is also said to inhibit the growth of tumors in breast, lung, and skin, and to be effective against prostate cancer amongst other types.

Turmeric should not be ingested in large quantities if you are pregnant or trying to conceive. Always consult your doctor about it if you have health problems.

---

2 glasses of smoothie

2 bananas

6 dates, pits removed

generous ⅓ cup / 100 ml coconut milk (without additives)

2 tbsp cold-pressed coconut oil

2 tbsp cocoa powder

1 tbsp turmeric

1¼ cups / 300 ml water

¾–1⅔ cups / 100–200 ml crushed ice (optional)

coconut flakes to decorate

Blend all the ingredients except the ice to a smooth consistency. Blend in the ice for a chilled smoothie. Serve in attractive glasses and sprinkle with coconut flakes.

PIÑA CHOCOLADA

Coconut oil is one of the world's healthiest oils. It is solid at room temperature but becomes liquid at around 75 °F / 24 °C. About 50 percent of the fat consists of lauric acid. The body converts this to monolauric acid that inhibits viruses, fungi, and bacteria. Coconut oil contains the highest proportion of lauric acid of all the foods in the world and in addition it contains caprylic acid, which boosts the growth of good intestinal bacteria, combats fungi, and kills parasites in the gut.

Coconut oil is suitable for cooking, smoothies, and desserts, and for skincare—I use coconut oil in place of skin cream. Always opt for organic, raw, cold-pressed, unbleached, unrefined, and undeodorized coconut oil. The list of ingredients should say that it is 100 percent coconut.

---

2 glasses of smoothie

1½ cups / 300 g pineapple (fresh or frozen)

generous ¾ cup / 200 ml water

generous ⅓ cup / 100 ml coconut milk
   (without additives)

2 tbsp cold-pressed coconut oil

2 tbsp cocoa powder

1 tbsp cocoa nibs

¾–1⅔ cups / 100–200 ml crushed ice
   (if you are using fresh pineapple)

coconut flakes to decorate

Blend all the ingredients except the ice together to a smooth consistency. Blend in the ice for a chilled smoothie. Serve in attractive glasses and sprinkle with coconut flakes.

Curious facts: A coconut palm flowers up to 13 times a year and the coconuts can therefore be harvested all year round. Every palm produces an average of 60 coconuts a year and 10,000 during its lifetime. The palms give us coconut oil, coconut water, coconut milk, coconut palm sugar, coconut flour, coconut nectar, coconut vinegar, coconut crisps, coconut flakes, and much more.

PEANUT CHOCOLATE

Peanut butter has become popular amongst joggers and fitness enthusiasts thanks to its high content of fiber, protein, healthy fats, minerals, vitamins, and antioxidants. In addition it has a satiating effect. Good peanut butter should be organically manufactured and consist of at least 99 percent peanuts. It should not contain anything else, with the possible exception of a little sea salt—however unsalted peanut butter is best for smoothies. There are many different varieties in the shops and some that contain both palm oil and sugar—beware of those!

---

2 glasses of smoothie

5 tbsp peanut butter

2 bananas, frozen

2 tbsp cocoa powder

1⅔ cups / 400 ml water

untreated peanuts for decoration

Blend all the ingredients to a smooth consistency. Serve in attractive glasses and sprinkle with crushed peanuts.

BUCKTHORN & CARROT

It is said that a single little buckthorn berry contains as much vitamin C as a whole orange. However the vitamin C content in buckthorn varies greatly per berry depending on the variety and the level of ripeness. Buckthorn contains vitamin B, which is rare in the plant kingdom and particularly important to vegetarians, and it also has B1, B2, B3 (niacin), B6, B9 (folic acid), pantothenic acid, biotin, vitamin E, and vitamin K.

2 glasses of smoothie

½ cup / 50 g buckthorn (fresh or frozen)

scant 1 cup / 100 g cashew nuts
   (or 5 tbsp cashew nut butter)

5–6 dates, pits removed

1¼ cups / 300 ml freshly pressed carrot juice

¾ cup / 100 ml coconut water

¾–1⅔ cups /100–200 ml ice (optional)

sweetener to taste

Blend the buckthorn, cashew nuts, and dates with the carrot juice and coconut water to a creamy consistency. Blend in the ice for a chilled smoothie. Taste and sweeten as required. Serve in large glasses with a couple of buckthorn berries on top.

COCONUT & PINEAPPLE

When the coconut is ripe the coconut water becomes viscous and milky—that is the actual coconut milk. The coconut milk that is on sale in cans in supermarkets is usually coconut extract diluted with water. Most cans say what proportion of the content is from the coconut and how much water has been added. Always buy unsweetened coconut milk without any additives.

Coconut milk is a creamy and tasty alternative to milk and cream in cooking. What is more, it is completely lactose free. The fat content may vary but is usually around 25 percent. Coconut milk is rich in potassium, iron, magnesium, and phosphorus, amongst other things.

You can produce smaller quantities of coconut milk yourself by blending grated coconut with water and then straining off the fruit flesh. Coconut milk freezes well in ice cube trays.

---

2 glasses of smoothie

½ pineapple (approx. 2 cups / 400 g frozen)

½ lime

1 banana

⅔ cup / 150 ml coconut milk

¾–1⅔ cups / 100–200 ml crushed ice (if you are using fresh fruit)

sweetener to taste

coconut or pineapple pieces for decoration

Divide the pineapple and remove the hard middle part. Press the lime, making sure that no seeds slip through as they can give a bitter taste. Blend all the ingredients except the ice to a smooth thick consistency. Sweeten to taste. Blend in the ice for a chilled smoothie. Serve with coconut or pineapple pieces.

BLUEBERRY, OATS, & VANILLA

Readymade oat milk is made from a mixture of oats and water which is then ground. In one stage of the process a number of naturally occurring enzymes are added. To obtain a milky consistency the insoluble fibers are removed, whilst the water-soluble fibers are retained. Finally the mixture is homogenized to form a smooth, even product. Oat milk is easy to make yourself—see the recipe on page 40.

2 glasses of smoothie

2 cups / 200 g blueberries, frozen

5 dates, pits removed

2 tsp chia seed

1⅔ cups / 400 ml oat milk

1 tsp vanilla extract

Blend all the ingredients to a smooth consistency. Serve in large glasses and decorate with a few blueberries.

BLACKBERRY, VANILLA YOGURT, & CINNAMON

A handful of blackberries contains almost half your daily requirement of fiber. Fiber keeps the gut going and helps the digestion to work. It also helps to regulate the blood sugar in the body. Blackberries are a good source of vitamins C and E, potassium, manganese, magnesium, iron, and vitamin K (amongst other things, this facilitates the absorption of calcium).

The dark color of blackberries comes from anthocyanins, a chemical coloring pigment and antioxidant substance that can reduce inflammation in the body and protect against free radicals, which otherwise can damage cells and contribute to cancer.

2 glasses of smoothie

2 cups / 200 g blackberries (fresh or frozen)

5 dates, pits removed

generous ¾ cup / 200 ml fresh pressed apple juice

generous ¾ cup / 200 ml vanilla soy yogurt

1 tsp ground cinnamon

2 tsp shelled hemp seed (optional)

Blend all the ingredients together to a smooth consistency. Decorate with a few blackberries.

PECAN NUT, DATE, & COCONUT WATER

Drinking coconut water has become extremely popular, both as a restorative after a hard session of exercise and as a little extra boost in smoothies. Coconut water is the clear liquid that is found in a young, green coconut. Coconut water consists of 95 percent water. The rest is nutrients and minerals such as vitamin B, vitamin C, phosphorus, calcium, and zinc. Coconut water is extra rich in potassium and is sometimes called "nature's own sports drink."

Coconut water should not be confused with coconut milk that is produced from the white flesh of a ripe, brown coconut. Coconut water freezes extremely well in ice cube trays and keeps for six months in the freezer.

---

2 glasses of smoothie

scant ½ cup / 50 g pecan nuts, untreated

7–8 dates

1 banana

1 tbsp chia seed

generous ¾ cup / 200 ml almond milk
(bought or homemade, recipe on page 40)

2 tbsp cocoa nibs

generous ¾ cup / 200 ml coconut water, frozen

Blend everything except the cocoa nibs and the coconut water to a creamy consistency. Add the cocoa nibs and coconut water, and blend to a chilled smoothie.

GOJI BERRY & COCONUT

Goji berries have proved to be one of the most nutritious foods found on earth. The goji berry is unique since among other things it contains 18 different amino acids, of which 7 are vital to life. In addition the goji berry is crammed full of important minerals, such as iron, calcium, zinc, selenium, copper, calcium, germanium, and phosphorus. It is also rich in vitamins B1, B2, B6, and E.

Did you know that goji berries contain five hundred times more vitamin C than oranges, three times more iron than spinach, and four times more antioxidants than cherries? Goji berries can be eaten as they are, or dried, or drunk as a juice.

---

2 glasses of smoothie

4 tbsp dried goji berries

1⅔ cups / 400 ml coconut water

4 tbsp coconut flakes, unsweetened

2 tbsp hemp seed

¾–1⅔ cups / 100–200 ml crushed ice

sweetener to taste

Leave the goji berries to soften in the coconut water for 5–10 minutes. Blend all the ingredients to a smooth consistency. Decorate with a few goji berries. A vitamin bomb!

RASPBERRY, COCONUT, & HEMP SEED

Hemp seed contains high levels of healthy polyunsaturated fatty acids and omega-3 and omega-6. The seeds consist of 25 percent protein and are rich in vital amino acids. They also contain high levels of calcium, magnesium, phosphorus, sulfur, carotene, iron, zinc, and vitamins E, C, B1, B2, B3, and B6.

Hemp seeds are found in several different forms: shelled, unshelled, and hemp protein powder, which works brilliantly as a natural protein boost.

---

2 glasses of smoothie

2½ cups / 300 g raspberries, frozen

generous ¾ cup / 200 ml coconut milk
(without additives)

2 tbsp coconut flakes, unsweetened

3 tbsp shelled hemp seed
(or 2 tbsp hemp protein powder)

3 tbsp sunflower seeds

Blend all the ingredients to a smooth consistency.

BLACKBERRY, LINSEED, & ALMOND

Linseed is incredibly nutritious. Among other things linseed contains vitamin B and minerals such as iron, phosphorus, potassium, calcium, zinc, and magnesium. Linseed is considered to be extra good for the stomach—like physalis, the seeds form a gelatinous layer that makes it easier for the stomach to work. Linseed is available whole or crushed. You should limit your intake—particularly of crushed linseed—some experts recommend no more than 2 tbsp a day.

---

2 glasses of smoothie

2 cups / 200 g blackberries, frozen

1¼ cups / 300 ml almond milk

2 tbsp almond butter

2 tbsp linseed

2 tbsp pumpkin seeds

1 tbsp vanilla sugar (optional)

sweetener to taste

Blend all the ingredients to a smooth consistency.

MACA-MOCHA WITH DATES

Traditionally the maca root has been used amongst other things for stress-related and hormonal problems, tiredness, malnutrition, and memory deficiencies, and to strengthen the immune system. However it is best known as an aphrodisiac to enhance fertility. The maca root contains significant quantities of amino acids, carbohydrates, and minerals such as calcium, zinc, magnesium, and iron. The maca root also contains vitamins B1, B2, B12, C, and E. Since the taste of maca powder is very distinct and easily dominates (it is slightly reminiscent of horseradish) it is safest to use a little at a time and taste as you go. It works well when mixed with other strong flavors.

2 glasses of smoothie

scant ½ cup / 50 g cashew nuts

6 dates, pits removed

½–1 tbsp maca powder

2 tbsp cocoa nibs

1 tbsp cocoa powder

1 tbsp coconut flakes

1 tbsp instant coffee powder

generous ¾ cup / 200 ml water

sweetener to taste

1⅔ cups / 200 ml crushed ice

coffee beans to decorate

Blend all the ingredients except the ice to a creamy consistency. Blend in the ice for a chilled smoothie. Serve in tall glasses with straws and decorate with a few coffee beans.

BANANA, COCONUT, & MAQUI BERRY

Maqui berries originally come from Patagonia in southern Chile. The berries rank highly on the so-called ORAC list that compares the antioxidant effects of foods. Maqui berries contain four times as much antioxidant as blueberries and twice as much as acai berries. That makes maqui berries an effective weapon against free radicals. In addition the berries protect the body's cells against oxidative stress and counteract premature aging. The antioxidants boost the immune system, break down inflammation, and help keep the blood sugar levels balanced. Maqui berries are crammed full of flavonoids, polyphenols, vitamins A, C, and E, and also the minerals calcium, iron, and potassium.

---

2 glasses of smoothie

2 bananas, frozen

1 cup / 100 g blueberries, frozen

1 tbsp maqui berry powder

generous ¾ cup / 200 ml coconut milk

2 tbsp agave syrup

Blend all the ingredients to a creamy consistency. Serve with a few blueberries on top.

AVOCADO, ALMOND, & ORANGE

Avocado is crammed full of healthy fats that can both protect against wrinkles and improve brain capacity. Throughout the ages the fruit has also been considered an aphrodisiac. In addition to its possible virility-enhancing effect and healthy monounsaturated fats, the avocado contains a lot of vitamin E that makes the skin smooth, soft, and healthy and at the same time gives the hair extra shine. The potassium content is also high, which helps to regulate blood pressure and is good for the muscles. There is also plenty of fiber, folic acid, vitamins A, B, and C, and magnesium in avocados.

---

2 glasses of smoothie

2 oranges

1 ripe avocado

2 tbsp almond butter

1¼ cups / 300 ml almond milk

Press the oranges. Take the pit out of the avocado and scoop out the flesh. Blend all the ingredients to a make a mild, creamy smoothie.

PRUNE & VANILLA YOGURT

Prunes are crammed with fiber and antioxidants. They get the digestion going and strengthen the immune system. Plums are rich in vitamins A, C, E, B2, B3, B6, calcium, iron, magnesium, and phosphorus.

Beware of eating too many prunes, especially in the beginning, otherwise there is a risk that the fiber will get the digestion going too well! Remember also to drink plenty of water when you eat foods rich in fiber, otherwise the effect can be the exact opposite.

---

2 glasses of smoothie

12 prunes, pits removed

2 tbsp dried goji berries

2 tbsp pecan nuts

2 tbsp hemp seed

1 tbsp linseed

generous ¾ cup / 200 ml freshly pressed apple juice

1⅔ cups / 400 ml vanilla soya yogurt

2 tbsp wheatgerm (optional)

Soak the prunes, goji berries, pecan nuts, hemp seed, and linseed in apple juice for 15–20 minutes. Blend to an even paste. Add the yogurt, wheatgerm if liked, and blend to a perfect breakfast smoothie that includes a serving of fiber.

SPINACH & APPLE

Spinach is a super food with a lot of antioxidants. The leaves are incredibly nutritious and contain among other things vitamins A, C, E, and K plus vitamin B9 (folic acid). Spinach is also rich in copper, iron, magnesium, calcium, chlorophyll, fiber, and other useful substances.

Spinach contains high levels of an inorganic nitrate that is believed to enhance the body's performance and muscle structure. Studies have shown that spinach makes the muscle cells' energy stations, the mitochondria, more efficient—which reduces the body's need for oxygen during physical exertion. Spinach is also thought to protect against cancer and high blood pressure, and to be good for those with stomach ulcers.

---

2 glasses of smoothie

generous ⅓ cup / 100 g fresh spinach, rinsed

1 banana

generous ¾ cup / 200 ml freshly pressed apple juice

juice of 1 lime

¾ cup / 100 ml crushed ice

1 tbsp spirulina (optional)

Blend all the ingredients into a creamy and nutritious smoothie. Boost with spirulina to make it even more nutritious.

CUCUMBER & GREEN PEA

Peas contain quantities of nourishment, proteins and vitamins—particularly vitamin B9 (folic acid) and the minerals iron and magnesium. In addition peas are rich in fiber, which is good for the stomach.

2 glasses of smoothie

½ cucumber

1 cup / 150 g green peas, frozen

1 tsp garlic powder (or 1 fresh clove)

2 tbsp hemp protein powder
  (or shelled hemp seed)

2 tbsp cold pressed olive oil

generous ¾ cup / 200 ml water

1 pinch sea salt

juice of half a lime (optional)

Cut the cucumber into pieces. Blend all the ingredients to a smooth consistency. Add lime juice for a sourer taste. Drink or eat as a cold soup.

MELON, PINEAPPLE, & SPINACH

Melon is part of the same family as pumpkin and cucumber. There are a lot of different kinds of melon, amongst them water melons and honeydew melons. Water melons usually have red flesh and dark brown seeds. There are also seedless varieties and some with yellow or orange flesh. Honeydew melons differ from water melons in having the seeds in the middle, which makes them easier to prepare. As a rule honeydew melons have smoother flesh, taste sweeter, and are more aromatic. Some other common kinds of melon are the musk melon, cantaloupe melon, charentais melon, and Gallia melon.

---

2 glasses of smoothie

½ honeydew melon

1 banana

½ cup / 100 g pineapple, frozen

1 tbsp hemp seed, shelled
  (or hemp protein powder)

3 tbsp / 50 g spinach

generous ⅓ cup / 100 ml water

Skin the melon and cut it into small pieces. Discard the seeds. Blend the melon pieces with the rest of the ingredients to make a creamy smoothie.

TIP! Try swapping the banana with an avocado.

GREEN PROTEIN BOMB

Celery has a high potassium content and is an excellent source of vitamins C and A, calcium, and protein. This vegetable is thought to protect against high blood pressure. The greatest quantities of vitamin C, calcium, and potassium are found in the green leaves. The leaves should be used within two days, otherwise they can wilt and the vitamins will disappear.

When you are buying celery look for straight, firm stalks that snap if you bend them and leaves that have not begun to turn yellow or shrivel. Keep celery in a closed container or wrapped in a plastic bag or damp cloth. Celery should not be kept too long at room temperature as its high water content means that it will shrivel quickly. If it begins to wilt, sprinkle it with water and put it back in the refrigerator to restore its crispness.

This recipe contains a lot of proteins and is perfect for recharging your batteries after a hard session of exercise.

---

2 glasses of smoothie

1 celery stalk

3 tbsp / 50 g baby spinach

3 tbsp hemp seed

3 tbsp almond butter

3 tbsp dried mulberries

1¼ cups / 300 ml almond milk

2 bananas, frozen

Cut the celery into pieces. Blend all the ingredients except the bananas to a smooth purée. Add the banana and blend to a chilled smoothie.

CUCUMBER, MINT, & NETTLE

In the sixteenth and seventeenth centuries the stinging nettle was used as a medicine for paralysis, rheumatism, scurvy, consumption, coughs, and (because the leaves are hairy!) baldness. Unfortunately the treatment often did not produce the desired result, even though the vitamins and minerals were undoubtedly a much needed addition to the diet. Today nettles are considered to have a purifying effect on the blood and are a general tonic for the body.

The first young spring leaves contain the highest proportion of nutrients. Nettles are chiefly rich in chlorophyll but also in beta-carotene, calcium, potassium, magnesium, iron, silicon, manganese, flavonoids, provitamin A, folic acid, and vitamins C, K, and B. Nettles in powder form are easy to use and can be obtained in health food shops.

---

2 glasses of smoothie

1 organic cucumber (400 g)

3 tbsp cashew nuts, raw

2 tbsp hemp seeds

3 tbsp/ 50 g chopped mint

3 tbsp / 50 g baby spinach

generous ¾ cup / 200 ml freshly pressed apple juice

1 tbsp nettle powder

juice of ½–1 lime

sweetener to taste

Cut the cucumber into pieces. Blend everything except the lime to make a green "vitamin bomb." Flavor with lime juice and sweetener.

TIP! If you want to try new flavors you can replace the nettle powder with wheatgrass powder or corn grass powder, available from well-stocked health food shops.

PEAR, BROCCOLI, & KIWIFRUIT

For vegans and others who do not eat dairy products, broccoli is valuable as a source of calcium. Calcium builds up the skeleton and is important for the normal functioning of the muscles. There is plenty of vitamins A, C, and K, folic acid, and fiber in broccoli. It also contains some vitamin B6, B1, B2, B3, and E, iron, potassium, magnesium, and zinc.

---

2 glasses of smoothie

2 ripe pears

5 broccoli florets (about 100 g)

1¼ cups / 300 ml freshly pressed apple juice

2 kiwifruit

1 banana, frozen

Cut up the pears and remove the cores. Cut the broccoli in pieces and blend with the pears and apple juice to a smooth purée. Add the kiwifruit and frozen banana and blend to a chilled smoothie. Do not blend it for too long as the black kiwifruit seeds can give a bitter taste if they are crushed in the blending.

GLOSSARY

ANTIOXIDANT. Protects the body against free radicals—that is, the residual products formed when the cells react with oxygen in the blood. A diet rich in fruit and vegetables is usually sufficient for us to absorb enough antioxidants. Vitamin C, vitamin E, beta-carotene, the co-enzyme Q, and selenium are particularly strong antioxidants. There is no evidence that extra antioxidants in the form of tablets can prevent disease.

BENZOIC ACID. Colorless crystalline substance with faintly sour characteristics. Benzoic acid is found in many kinds of fruit and vegetables and acts as a natural preservative. Lingon berries, cranberries, and cloudberries contain such high levels of benzoic acid that they can cause allergic reactions.

BETA-CAROTENE. A preliminary stage (provitamin) of vitamin A (retinol) that occurs chiefly in vegetables. Found in carrots, mangos, and kale amongst other things. In the body beta-carotene is converted into vitamin A.

BIODYNAMIC CULTIVATION. This is a form of organic cultivation in which factory-made, easily soluble fertilizers and chemical pesticides are avoided. Biodynamic agriculture also comprises a cyclical theory that is comparable with self-sufficient organic agriculture. The technique endeavors to create a complete cycle on a small scale and build up and reinforce the organic systems in the earth. Composting and grassland cultivation are two important methods.

CAROTENES. Natural, yellow to yellowish red colorants that are found in carrots, mangos, papaya, and egg yolks amongst other things.

CELL. The smallest building block in all living things: from bacteria and fungi to plants and people. Most cells are small and can be seen only through a microscope. It takes two billion cells to build up a fruit. New cells are formed by old ones dividing. Some scientists think that all living things on earth derive from one cell or a small number of prototype cells that lived 3.5 billion years ago.

DIETARY FIBER. This is chiefly found in vegetables, fruit, whole grains, seeds, and nuts. It helps to keep blood sugar levels stable and lower cholesterol. Extra fiber supplements such as oat germ, wheatgerm, linseed, psyllium seeds, and chia seed keep the body balanced. It is good to eat them in the morning. Dietary fiber cannot be broken down by the gut and is therefore not absorbed by the body. It slows down the digestion and gives a feeling of satiety without adding calories. It also means that food passes through the gut more quickly, which reduces the risk of constipation. Dietary fiber is thought to provide some protection against cancer of the large intestine.

ENZYMES. Proteins that help in chemical reactions in the body. For example the enzyme myosin is needed for the muscles to contract. Another enzyme is pepsin, which breaks down the proteins in food. Enzymes are vital to all organisms and they are also used in washing powder (for example to dissolve stains).

ETHYLENE GAS. Given off by certain fruit, they can cause other fruit and vegetables to ripen more quickly. Apples, pears, melons, bananas, peaches, nectarines, plums, apricots, and tomatoes give off a lot of ethylene gas.

FREE RADICALS or RADICALS. Occur when the cells use oxygen to obtain energy. This is perfectly normal and is regulated by various enzymes in the body. Through our food we take in antioxidants that neutralize the radicals. Carotene, vitamin C, and vitamin E are examples of antioxidants. Normally the body takes care of all free radicals that are formed, but the balance may be disrupted by—for instance—medicines, radiation, or a deficiency of certain substances. If there is an excess of radicals they may attack the cells and cause damage. It is thought that this may be one of the reasons why the body ages.

LACTOSE INTOLERANCE. This occurs when the enzyme lactase is missing from the small intestine and makes it difficult to tolerate milk and dairy products. Some sufferers can eat sour milk cultures and yogurt since these contain less lactose than normal, fresh milk. People who are lactose intolerant often get diarrhea when they eat dairy products. Lactose is also called milk sugar. In some countries a high proportion of people are lactose intolerant.

MINERALS. The human body needs about 20 different minerals to survive but only in very small quantities. The mineral we need most is calcium, which is found in the skeleton and the teeth. Other minerals include phosphorus, potassium, sodium, and magnesium. Substances of which we need only a very little are called trace elements. These include iron, iodine, zinc, and selenium. If we eat a varied diet we usually take in enough minerals. Vitamins do not count as minerals.

ORGANIC CULTIVATION. A cultivation technique based on renewable resources that are close to the farm, for example cow dung. By fertilizing the soil you build up the earth's fertility. No artificial fertilizer or chemical pesticides are used, instead plant varieties with their own resistance that grow more slowly are cultivated. Genetically modified organisms (GMOs) are not permitted in organic production.

OXIDATION. This is a chemical reaction. When a piece of apple turns brown this is because the substances in the apple react with the acid in the air and oxidize.

PESTICIDES. There are both biological pesticides (the natural enemies of the pests) and chemical pesticides (herbicides, fungicides, and insecticides). These are mainly used in agriculture, horticulture, and forestry. Pesticides facilitate intensive agriculture without loss of crops and since the middle of the twentieth century have contributed to a major increase in world food production. However their use entails considerable risks to health and in many countries their use is controlled by the government.

PRESERVATIVE. Substance that extends the shelf-life of food by preventing the external effects of micro-organisms, plants, animals, and chemical substances. Preservatives protect against the formation of mold and fermentation, for example. Benzoic acid, which is found in lingon berries and cloudberries, and sorbic acid, which is found in rowan berries, are good examples of natural preservatives. In addition there are many other preservative food additives, many of them approved for specific governments.

PROBIOTICS. These are living micro-organisms in the form of bacteria cultures. Probiotics are thought to be very important to the immune system, bodyweight, throat health, and even the functions of the brain. They help the body to recreate useful bacteria that fight disease-causing organisms in the intestine. Probiotics are often used to prevent diarrhea, gas, and cramps caused by antibiotics. Probiotics can be taken as tablets or capsules, or in the form of foods to which the organisms have been added, for example yogurt and fruit drinks. Read also about kombucha on page 38.

VITAMINS. Substances that are vital to human beings but of which we need only small quantities. Since the body cannot form vitamins itself we have to obtain them by eating a balanced diet.

Humans need 12 different vitamins. They are usually divided into fat-soluble and water-soluble vitamins. Fat-soluble ones are vitamins A, D, E, and K. Water-soluble ones are the various B vitamins (B1, B2, B6, B12, niacin, folic acid, biotin), and vitamin C.

Vitamin A is needed for vision and for the body's defense against infections. Vitamin D is needed to keep the skeleton strong. Vitamin E is needed amongst other things for the body's defense against free radicals. Vitamin K is needed for the blood to be able to coagulate ("set") when there is a wound. Vitamin C is also called ascorbic acid. The body needs it to form connective tissue and take up iron from food. The immune system is also strengthened by vitamin C. Most vitamin C is found in fruit and vegetables.

INDEX

Light & fruity smoothies **42**

Apricot, raspberry, & chamomile 89

Blueberry, blackberry, & beets 82

Blueberry, coconut, & acai berry 94

Blueberry, raspberry, & goji berry 81

Buckthorn, mango, & strawberry 46

Carrot, orange, & cayenne pepper 42

Carrot, pineapple, & goji berries 70

Grape, strawberry, & lucuma 90

Kiwifruit & mango 54

Lingon berry, mango, & acai berry 86

Lingon berry, orange, & goji berry 78

Mango, orange, & rose hip 53

Nectarine, raspberry, & mulberry 74

Orange & banana 62

Pineapple, goji berries, & redcurrants 73

Pineapple, papaya, & lucuma 85

Pineapple & strawberry 57

Pomegranate & grapefruit 65

Raspberry & mango 93

Raspberry & pear 66

Redcurrants & mango 58

Rose hip, pineapple, & papaya 49

Strawberry, kombucha, & mulberry 77

Strawberry & chamomile 45

Strawberry & chili 61

Tropical fruit 69

Watermelon, raspberry, & mint 50

Rich & creamy smoothies **97**

Almond chocolate with banana & vanilla. 97

Avocado, almond, & orange 125

Banana, coconut, & maqui berry 122

Blackberry, linseed, & almond 118

Blackberry, vanilla yogurt, & cinnamon 110

Blueberry, oats, & vanilla 109

Buckthorn & carrot 105

Chocolate, date, & turmeric 98

Coconut & pineapple 106

Goji berry & coconut 114

Maca-Mocha with dates 121

Peanut chocolate 102

Pecan nut, date, & coconut water 113

Piña chocolada 101

Prune & vanilla yogurt 126

Raspberry, coconut, & hemp seed 117

Green smoothies **129**

Cucumber, mint, & nettle 137

Cucumber & green pea 130

Green protein bomb 134

Melon, pineapple, & spinach 133

Pear, broccoli, & kiwifruit 138

Spinach & apple 129

Abbreviations and Quantities

1 oz = 1 ounce = 28 grams
1 lb = 1 pound = 16 ounces 1
1 cup = approx. 5–8 ounces* (see below)
1 cup = 8 fluid ounces = 250 milliliters (liquids)
2 cups = 1 pint (liquids) = 15 milliliters (liquids)
8 pints = 4 quarts = 1 gallon (liquids)
1 g = 1 gram = 1/1000 kilogram = 5 ml (liquids)
1 kg = 1 kilogram = 1000 grams = 2¼ lb
l l = 1 liter = 1000 milliliters (ml) = 1 quart
125 milliliters (ml) = approx. 8 tablespoons = ½ cup
1 tbsp = 1 level tablespoon = 15–20 g* (depending on density) = 15 milliliters (liquids)
1 tsp = 1 level teaspoon = 3–5 g * (depending on density) = 5 ml (liquids)

*The weight of dry ingredients varies significantly depending on the density factor, e.g. 1 cup of flour weighs less than 1 cup of butter. Quantities in ingredients have been rounded up or down for convenience, where appropriate. Metric conversions may therefore not correspond exactly. It is important to use either American or metric measurements within a recipe.

The purpose of the recipes and advice in this book is simply to give guidance on quality nutrition and how to increase your energy. If you have a medical condition you should consult your doctor.

© Eliq Maranik and Stevali Production
Original Title: *Hälsosmoothies – boosta din kropp med vitaminer, mineraler och antioxidanter!*
Original ISBN: 978-91-86287-50-4

Photography: Eliq Maranik and Stefan Lindström, with the exception of
pages 8, 20, 23, 31, 32, 41 iStockphoto.com
Art Director: Eliq Maranik
Graphic design: Eliq Maranik and Alan Maranik / Stevali Production
Editing: Anton Borgström and Eva Stjerne Ord & Form

© for this English edition: h.f.ullmann publishing GmbH
Special edition

Translation from Swedish: Julie Martin in association with First Edition Translations Ltd, Cambridge, UK
Editing and typesetting: First Edition Translations Ltd, Cambridge, UK

Project management for h.f.ullmann: Rabea Rittgerodt, Isabel Weiler
Overall responsibility for production: h.f.ullmann publishing GmbH, Potsdam, Germany

Printed in Italy, 2014
ISBN 978-3-8480-0715-8

10 9 8 7 6 5 4 3 2 1
X IX VIII VII VI V IV III II I

www.ullmann-publishing.com
newsletter@ullmann-publishing.com
facebook.com/ullmann.social

MIX
Papier aus verantwortungsvollen Quellen
Paper from responsible sources
FSC® C006866